WHEN GOLIATH DOESN'T FALL

JODY CONRAD

BEACON HILL PRESS
OF KANSAS CITY

Copyright 2008
by Jody Conrad and Beacon Hill Press of Kansas City

ISBN-13: 978-0-8341-2357-1
ISBN-10: 0-8341-2357-6

Cover Design: Chad A Cherry
Interior Design: Sharon Page

All Scripture quotations not otherwise designated are from the *New American Standard Bible*® (NASB®), © copyright The Lockman Foundation 1960, 1962, 1963, 1968, 1971, 1972, 1973, 1975, 1977, 1995. Used by permission.

Scripture quotations marked NIV are from the Holy Bible, *New International Version*®. Copyright © 1973, 1978, 1984 by International Bible Society. Used by permission of Zondervan Publishing House. All rights reserved.

Scripture quotation marked KJV is from the King James Version.

Library of Congress Cataloging-in-Publication Data

Conrad, Jody, 1968-
 When Goliath doesn't fall / Jody Conrad.
  p. cm.
 Includes bibliographical references.
 ISBN-13: 978-0-8341-2357-1 (pbk.)
 ISBN-10: 0-8341-2357-6 (pbk.)
 1. Prayer—Christianity. I. Title.

 BV220.C57 2008
 248.3'2—dc22

2008000146

For all those who see no reason to hope . . .
and do so anyway.

God is not ashamed to be called their God.
—Heb. 11:16

CONTENTS

Acknowledgments 7

1. Wild Roses: Knowing He Sees You 9
2. Into Places of Obscurity: Knowing His Voice 19
3. Stars from the Deep: Facing Slander 29
4. Silent Night: Facing Limited Resources 43
5. An Alabaster Jar: Facing the Loss of a Child 53
6. Broken for Vows: Facing Injury in the Line of Duty 65
7. An Altar for the Deep: Facing Terror 77
8. Code Red: Facing Tragedy on the Mission Field 93
9. Pathfinders: Facing Health Issues 111
10. Spectacles of Faith: The Hebrews 11 Hall of Famers 129
11. In Domino Fashion: The Hope of the Habakkuk Heart 153
12. In Defiance: Knowing the Distance He Ran for You 167

Afterword 181

Scriptures of Hope 183

Works Cited 189

ACKNOWLEDGMENTS

Behind every writer is a host of people who make it possible for him or her to produce a book. My first thanks goes to the Author of Life. He promises to complete what He has begun in each of us. Into each chapter of my life He has brought people who have impacted my life in ways they'll never fully know. In them He has shown me a snapshot of himself. In them my own faith is strengthened.

First is my husband, Ron: your quiet strength makes me feel safe.

To my sons, Ryan and Brent: the thought of you fills my heart with joy. Thanks for being good sports by eating all those grilled cheese sandwiches because I needed to get back to writing.

To my parents, Monte and Kathy and Joe and Leona: your unconditional love means the world.

To my sisters, Lori, Julie, Patti, Crystal, and Vonnie: I treasure each of you.

To my brothers, Wayne, Dan, Mark, and Tom: thanks for standing up for me when I needed it most in this life.

To Fred Crowell: you led me to the Lord. How do I thank you?

To Pastor Nyholm, Pastor Grant, and Pastor Zimmerman: your love for the Word kept me coming back.

To Von and Judy: thanks for keeping our heads above the storm waters.

To Les Stobbe, my agent: thank you for seeing a writer behind the barley and chalkdust.

To all the people who have allowed me to paint a portrait of their faith in this book: I hope I did you justice. Thank you for your willingness to share your most difficult valley. I hope to tread this earth with as much grace.

And finally, thank you to Judi and Barry and all the editors and publicists at Beacon Hill Press of Kansas City; you're creative, professional, and a blast to work with!

1
WILD ROSES
KNOWING HE SEES YOU

*With each trial can be heard
the fervency of heaven's loom.*
—Jody

HER LUNGS BURNED—not from the cancer but from the extra mile of running she was determined to put in that day. *One more mile. Help me, Lord, go one more mile.* With each step the piece of gravel in her running shoe continued its roll across the bottom of her foot. She pressed on. Nothing would stand in the way of reaching her goal: she had her eyes on the fencepost up ahead, and that's where she would stop.

Almost there, she said to herself. She enjoyed the country with its roadside banks of wild roses. Clumped in masses, they were a moving screen of eye-popping yellow as she jogged. Meandering along untamed, they spilled over rocky banks, dotting the hillsides with a grandeur that easily surpassed that of any well-groomed flower bed.

They have a wild faith, she thought. Looking at them, one would think it impossible that such beauty could spring from soil-scarce crags. Even the abandoned rails racing parallel alongside the road were no match for their far-reaching blooms. The yellow beauties stretched out across the tracks. Using them like a trellis, with wild faith they climbed the countryside.

A better time than yesterday, she said to herself as she neared the fencepost. Panting, she glanced from the countryside to her wristwatch, slowed to a walk, stopped, and put her hands on her hips. It felt good to breathe deeply. She bent down and untied her laces just far enough to slip her heel out and allow the annoying piece of gravel to tumble out of her shoe.

For the last 10 years, cancer had railed against her from the gates of hell. It had tried to contain her, pull her into its soil-sparse crags, and truncate her stamina for living—but she had a wild faith. She kept crawling back out of hospital beds. Here she was, the day after chemotherapy, out jogging! In the back of her mind, she knew it was likely that her type of cancer would have the last word—highly likely. No doctor needed to tell her that. Her bones could feel the disease's tailgating fury.

But not today, she said to herself as she tied her laces back up.

Getting to her feet, she hurled the piece of gravel. Like the sound of a start gun at the race tracks, it pinged against the nearby rails before bouncing into some ryegrass. *Not today.* And with that she took off like a bullet, back down the graveled road, the wind in her blonde hair. She had things to do. She needed to get home, fix dinner, help the kids with their homework, and then get to choir practice. Nothing, not even a little terminal illness, was going to keep her from singing in the choir Sunday morning. Down the road, alongside the wild roses, she raced, humming to herself one of the songs they would be going over at practice. No one had slung the rock of faith farther than Karyn, nor as eloquently.

And yet with the passing of the yellow blooms that season—she was gone.

* * *

I know he's out there. She had no doubt he was watching over her. Her long brown hair graced the back of the sack-like dress she was wearing, the humble material still unable to hide her becoming frame as she strolled through the peasant village along the worn path. Every now and then a few wispy strands of hair would catch the afternoon breeze and dance around her tender cheekbones. She smiled. Her blue eyes held a secret no one else in the village knew. She swung her basket, dreamily unaware of the bustling commoners going about their daily routines. It was fall. Men chopped wood, women prepared large vats of boiling water, young girls hung out laundry, and little boys darted in and out through the huts lining the path, playing their favorite Scottish games. Clumsily, one bumped into her. She patted his head of unruly hair before he ran off.

It was the year of our Lord 1270. She reached up and felt for the brown cloth tucked under her collar out of sight; it draped loosely around her neck beneath her clothes. She smiled and thought of him. In the heavily wooded hills of the highlands that surrounded their village, they had been secretly married. Every married woman in the village wore the brown scarf. Recently, however, women wore it with a fair amount of trepidation.

England's self-indulging King Edward had sent forth an edict throughout the land that forced the hand of all Scottish brides into a night with his royal subjects before giving themselves in marriage to their betrothed. The idea repulsed every woman and sent waves of rage through the hearts of every Scotsman. For that reason, the two of them had decided to buck the king's rule and get married in secret. Keeping their marriage and love for one another from the other villagers had been challenging.

She could always feel him looking at her. She glanced up from the worn path. There he was, standing behind a birch tree just outside the village. Her heart skipped a beat. From his warrior frame he stared at her. She blushed.

"When can we meet again?" he whispered to her. She held his eyes and kept walking so as not to arouse the suspicion of any of the villagers or the nearby foot soldier standing at his post.

"Soon," she mouthed. He continued to mirror her every step, passionately keeping a safe distance away. His hazel eyes smiled back. She loved the way he held her with those eyes. He drew closer, nearly brushing her hand.

They could sense their antics stirring the curiosity of the foot soldier. For her protection, he withdrew and watched from a distance as she continued dreamily along the meandering path. It took a natural bend and she disappeared from his sight. A few steps into the turn, she bumped straight into the brassy buttons of a red coat. The stubbly grin of the soldier told her she was in danger.

He peered intently at the corner of the brown scarf now peeking out above the line of her collar. "You're married!" he said half-surprised. He grabbed her by the arm. "Captain," he yelled. "We've got ourselves a rabbit!" She could hear the base hoops and hollers of the soldiers making their way toward her from their posts. The soldier holding her arm tried his best to wrestle her to the ground, but she fought back, biting the corner of his earlobe. It was enough to loosen his grip and recoil him into yelps of pain.

Just then, out of nowhere, came a pair of flying fists. It was her husband. He was always close by. He leveled two of the guards in a matter of minutes before placing her safely on horseback. "Meet me at the Tweed Bridge!" he shouted as he swatted the steed's hindquarters and sent her galloping out of camp. By now, other soldiers were running toward the brawl. With quickness, he dodged their lunges and made his way out of camp, too, and up into the dense forests of highlands.

"Murron! Murron!" he called as he ran. The birch trees swallowed his lonely echo. He stopped. His heart dropped. "She was to meet me here!" he said aloud in disbelief. Like a wild dog, he continued his search for her. "She should have been here by now!" he said, panicking. "Murron!" trailed his yearning shouts through the dense brush. He guessed he would double back to the village and find her. Nothing would stand in his way. "Murron!" he called, jumping from boulder to boulder. Like a panther, he skirted through the tall brush to find her; with his heart raging, he made his way back toward the village.

She, in fact, had not made it out of camp. From the top of a thatched roof, along the edge of camp, one of the foot soldiers had jumped, knocking her from the horse. Grabbing her by the ankles, he dragged her feet-first back through the village. She pawed at the ground, desperately grasping at the passing grasses. Her resistance was no match for his brute strength. Like a rag doll, she bumped along the dirt path behind him to the center of the village where the captain stood waiting to make an example of her before the rest of the "no-good commoners." At his feet she was thrown.

Clutching his newfound prey, he stood her up by the hair as if to display her to the gathering crowd before tying her to a pole. Mud splattered up and down the front of her dress and mixed with the blood that dripped from her nose. Defiantly, she clenched the handfuls of earth in her bound hands and ignored his presence. It infuriated him. He grabbed her chin and forced her gaze toward him. Her eyes told him that he could take her life, but he would never have her respect.

"This is what happens to those who make a fool of the king and his subjects!" the captain shouted as he raised his knife to her throat. She scanned the highlands behind her accusers.

He was out there. She knew the injustice of this day would not end without *his* answer to it all. She envisioned the look in his eyes. He would be aflame at her mistreatment. Whether he came now or later, she knew he would have the last word. The knife blade at her throat was no match for her fierce confidence in his coming.

She could feel the heat of his warrior heart rising in her own blood with every passing minute, and it gave her a peace. *If he doesn't make it in time to save me,* she thought as she scanned the hills one last time, *I know he won't let my death be in vain.* In one quick movement came the slit of the captain's blade. Pebbles slipped from her bound hands. Falling to the ground, she was gone.

* * *

Down through the ages the faithful have faced unbeatable Goliaths. Their antagonists have been as formidable and ruthless as those in Mel Gibson's movie *Braveheart.* Perhaps, you've found yourself unfairly pushed into the crags of life by one of them and been made to live in intolerable conditions. Maybe, no matter how much you pray, your situation remains depressingly unchanged as you feel the knife blade of injustice at your throat. Maybe you're battling cancer. Maybe you've buried a child. Maybe you've just been dragged by your hair down a slandering path that has destroyed your credibility, your reputation, or a well-earned career.

In any event, you've been hogtied by an unbeatable Goliath. While you accept and understand that life's not fair, you also understand you serve a God who is bigger than any circumstance, a God who can rescue "Daniels" from lions' dens and keep flames at bay, a God who helps the faithful pull in the ramp and set sail just before the floodwaters rise.

If He can cause arks to set sail on maiden voyages from deserts and make Goliaths fall with one little pebble, surely He can fell *your* Goliath. So why *hasn't* He? With great faith, you've slung the rock.

What's this all about, God?

While we're sure heaven rejoices in the faith of those who pick up pebbles, slay Goliaths, and give the living God the praise for miraculous deliverances and interceding favor, we fail to understand that it is the sound of praise when Goliath *doesn't* fall that stirs the heavens into awestruck silence. Only the Habakkuk heart holds that kind of praise. It is a heart that captivates heaven.

Whether delivered from its circumstances or not, this heart *still* worships. With cancer in its lungs, it still sings. At a son's graveside, it keeps its faith. With the tread marks of slander down its back, it still offers up praise.

And when such a rare song ripples the heavens, celestial beings draw still to listen and hear the piercing melody of the Habakkuk heart as it scans the hillside for its God and helper and says, *Should you come today and rescue me or not, still I will be yours! Somewhere in the highlands you do see me, and I know you will right every wrong. In your time, you will accomplish what concerns me. This enemy will not have the last word, and neither will I dishonor you by writhing against its shears.*

These are the stories of the Habakkuk heart, the kind of heart that enthralls the heavens, for it is a heart that worships God with a wild faith. It is a heart that worships God even w*hen Goliath doesn't fall.*

> Though the yield of the olive should fail And the fields produce no food, Though the flock should be cut off from the fold And there be no cattle in the stalls, Yet I will exult the LORD *(Hab. 3:17-18).*

2
INTO PLACES OF OBSCURITY:
KNOWING HIS VOICE

On blades of grass string jewels of dew,
suspended pearls;
Hidden treasures for morning beggars.
—Jody

CAVE: A HOME OR DWELLING PLACE. It was dark. He was weary. He had been chased by Jezebel all day. Hurricane winds tore at the entrance of his gloomy cave. Elijah stood and listened. *It sounds like this place might be torn apart,* he said to himself as he wrapped his face in his mantle and made his way to the cave's entrance. The winds were strong and mighty, like his God. However, he sensed they were not from His hand. Suddenly, the ground beneath his sandals began to quake, throwing him from his footing. He lunged for the wall of the cave and hung on. The powerful quake knocked him several yards back into the cave.

He pulled his knees to his chest and covered his head with his hands. And then it was over. He looked up. Loose pebbles rolled to the edges of his sandals. *That was a big one.* But something told him the earthquake wasn't from the Lord either. He served a mighty God, but his God could speak just as loudly through the humble things of earth. His God was a mighty king who he felt would soon come into this world. He didn't know how, or exactly when, but he knew He would come, mighty and humble all at the same time.

Lord, I know just by the way you speak to your servant that you will come both as a mighty king and kneeling king, he prayed as he stood up and brushed the dust from his sleeves. At the entrance of the cave came a red glow. He coughed and made his way toward it but had to stop. Outside, flames swept by, licking the entrance and scorching everything in sight. With the heat pressing into the cave, he took a step back. *This isn't you, Lord.*

After the fire passed, Elijah went and stood just outside the entrance of the cave. Darkness engulfed the landscape, a gray smell blanketed the air, and beneath his sandals the earth smoldered. A gentle breeze swept across his face; it was the voice of his mighty God. He would recognize it anywhere. *Thank you for being here,* Elijah said, exhaling.

In this hurricane-swept, post-9-11 world, it's sometimes difficult to hear the voice of God. But whether or not we hear Him in those moments of earthquaking sorrow, perhaps the greater tragedy is that we fail to hear His voice in the gentle breezes of the everyday.

* * *

My husband pulls out of the driveway, and the Sunday morning routine begins. I slip my Bible into my handbag and dig around for a stick of gum with hopes of fumbling across a tube of lipstick while I'm at it. Instantly from the back seat comes the predictable "Mom, can I have a stick of gum?"

"Me, too," pipes another voice. I hand two sticks back.

"Did you get your Bibles?" I ask. Their replies are lost in my searching thoughts as to whether or not I unplugged the curling iron in the bathroom.

"Honey," my husband breaks in, "did you fill the car up with gas?"

"I have youth group tonight—don't forget," our oldest says, conveniently interrupting.

"Did you feed your pup?" answers his dad. And with that the van comes to a stop in the church parking lot where we all pile out.

"Don't slam the do—" trails my phantom request behind our boys who are already bounding down the church sidewalk toward the basement doors. My husband and I slip through the front doors and wrestle our coats around the attached hangers in the foyer. As we head to the activity center where our adult Sunday School class meets, I wonder why every church I've ever been in has such hangers.

We spot two folding chairs and quickly take our seats. *Was there some sort of church hanger heist I didn't know about?* We open our Bibles, and class begins in prayer. Nestling into the shoulder of my husband, I tug my thoughts away from the distraction of unplugged curling irons, low gas tanks, and church hangers.

Help me to hear your voice, Lord, I pray. Our study is in the Book of John, where Jesus talks to the woman at the well. As the teacher begins explaining the social barriers surrounding the Bible story, my thoughts slip onto the text before me. I imagine Jesus approaching the woman.

* * *

From the afternoon shadows a figure emerges on the desert's horizon line. His step is masked by the desert's mirage-like heat. As He nears the village's only well, He takes up a trailing slack of rope snaking several yards away from the well wall. Gently, He pulls with a last lumbering tug.

The quick ascent of the winched bucket causes a woman who has come to draw water to turn her attention from the well's black hole. *I wonder who's come to put me in my place,* she thinks as she looks up over her shoulder and squints into the noonday sun. Surprisingly, she finds the smiling eyes of an olive-skinned stranger. He draws closer.

Skimming within inches of her shoulder, He reaches over the knee-high rock wall and lifts the rickety, wooden bucket of water from the well's crude wench, only to set it next to her water pot on the stone wall. Then He takes a seat himself.

Taken aback, the woman stares at Him. Soon the nagging desert heat and her thirst remind her of the reason she has come, and her curious gaze loosens from His and shifts back to her empty water jar near the bucket. For a moment she thinks about snatching up her jar and hightailing it out of this stranger's presence. But there's something about Him that causes her to linger. There's no judgment in His eyes. She doesn't remember the last time she has been given a look devoid of judgment, and that alone keeps her from leaving. She lingers.

Then the voice of God speaks. And of all the things He could have said—the Living Water asks her for a drink.

He puts her at ease and makes himself vulnerable, at the mercy of her water jar. His humility moves her. His gentle strength calls this woman in the throes of obscurity to withdraw from the cave of her heart, from the place where she's lived shielded from the world's condemnation, from the cave that has kept her safe from the world's harsh opinions and shattering slander. There in the desert, she is quenched by the gentle voice of God. It is not like the voices of her world.

This voice is full of humility and asks instead of takes. It is a voice that seeks to expose the darkness of her hidden heart for no other reason than to free it. It is a voice that lends to her a dignity she has never known. It is the voice of the infinite God tucking and rolling himself into a finite cup of water—something her trodden soul can put a handle to.

He drinks from the cup she offers, and somehow His act of pointed humility draws back the veil between two worlds and imparts salvation to her thirsty soul. Filled with a cleansing excitement, she wraps her face in her mantle and scurries from the well. His admonition to go and sin no more merely punctuates the lilt in her step as she hurries unburdened back to her village to share with others her encounter with Christ. Though in her haste she has forgotten her water jar, her desert shadow makes no indication that she'll return for it. No longer thirsty, she hurries, silhouetted against the siren red of a setting sun. She can hear the transforming voice of her mighty, kneeling King.

* * *

The slamming of the double doors in the back of the activity center jolts my thoughts from the scene at the well. I don't need to turn my head to know who it is. The quick pitter-patter across the carpeted floor tells me. As he rounds the front row of folding chairs, my suspicion is confirmed: it's three-year-old Isaac Erickson, who's made another daring escape from the nursery. He manages at least one escape every month or so, and this must be his Sunday.

He stops dead center in front of the first row of folding chairs and looks at all of us seated in the adult Sunday School class. He doesn't move. He just stands there smiling. Then he smiles some more. Soon the double doors slam again. This time it's the heavy footsteps that tell us who it is.

Isaac still doesn't move. Perhaps he knows he's in the clear until his father is within three steps. He just stands there with those rosy cheeks and that heavenly grin. Though we know there are no favorites in the Body of Christ, we secretly give Isaac that honor in our hearts.

Born with Down's syndrome, Isaac is supposedly more challenged than the rest of us. But everyone has come to know that Isaac is the least challenged of us all. We look forward to his escapes from the nursery. We hunger for that unmistakable grin he gives so freely. For a brief moment as he stands before us, we all feel as if—well, as if we're special and *worth* being grinned at! He entices us to crawl out of our caves.

We become putty in his hands as he somehow takes us back to the sandboxes of our childhoods where we first learned to smile. We sit fixed on his genuineness, and we run our hands through purity and innocence that beckon us to live a life free of self absorption, free of the worry of what others think of us. In that smile and those rosy cheeks, we hear the call to abandon the tactics of adulthood and repent of self-protectionism. Before us stands the absence of false pretense, and it's refreshing. It's a depth we just can't stop gazing into.

All too soon the time in the sandbox is up. Isaac's dad is within the perimeter of radar. And as quickly as that heavenly boy pitter-pattered into the room, he pitter-patters out through the double doors with Dad in pursuit. We close in prayer and hope that he'll escape from the nursery again soon so that we can once more hear the voice of our kneeling king in the sermon of his little-boy grin.

Perhaps it's there in the humble that He's been speaking to us all along. It's in the ordinary that He tucks His splendor: in the manger, in a wildflower, in the unknown mechanism that causes a salmon to spawn, in the order atop a funny dandelion, in the gentle breeze that graced Elijah's face. All are servant reminders that if we seek Him, we'll find Him where the world doesn't lend its applause. We'll find Him in the gentle breezes of the everyday.

Mighty Kneeling King

To cup Jupiter in the palm of your hand,
Or shoebox a moonbeam with the starlight above,

To balance a mountain range upon the back of a lily pad,
Or kite by hand the Milky Way across the evening sky,

To pour a whale into a Mason jar,
Or bundle a forest into a cocoon,

To pocket the Grand Canyon,
Or build a coliseum upon a blade of grass,

To transport an army on the wing of a butterfly,
Or moor a boat in a puddle of rain,

To hide the ocean within a thimble,
Or cradle in a teacup the pyramids of Egypt

Impossible and absurd condescensions are they all,
but none so as the reality that my God and Savior
would cookie-cutter himself into the keyhole of my heart,
just so I might know His great love for me.

And, though no mortal should be allowed
To cradle its Creator in a manger
Or temple the living God,

May the hearts of earth receive such a mighty and humble King!

—Jody and Brent Conrad

3
STARS FROM THE DEEP

FACING SLANDER

In the epicenter of life it's sometimes difficult to see past the first few rings of turbulence to the shoreline where heaven stands skipping pebbles, top-quilting dull waters into works of art.

—Jody

IT WAS OFFICIAL. It would take place on the 13th day of the 12th month. The red seal confirmed it, for it was the signature mark of none other than King Ahasuerus. A copy of the edict had been issued as law in the outlying provinces and posted on every scrub tree in the hillside districts. Travelers were sure to see it—and if by some chance they didn't, they would no doubt see the upheaval it was causing. The city of Susa was in a state of confusion.

Beneath the tree's outstretched limbs, she pressed further into the tense crowd that had gathered under the grove of trees along the knobby hill. She pulled the veil close around her face. *I can't let anyone find out who I am.* In front of her, bobbing heads weaved back and forth, straining for a closer look at the scrolled parchment nailed to the tree's knotted trunk. She craned her neck to see the signature at the bottom of the weather-torn scroll. She would recognize that signature anywhere!

She gasped in unbelief. *It was true!* Pulling her veil over her mouth and nose, she turned and made her way out of the sobbing crowd and its unfolding wails. She felt sick to her stomach. She and her servants had fasted for three days, hoping it wasn't true. But her uncle Mordecai had been right. The destruction of the Jewish people—her own people—had been ordered by none other than her husband, the king.

It can't be! I know my king's heart. This is not his doing. But who? She hurried back against the setting sun to her hidden chariot. *Of course! This has all the earmarks of*

Susa's most prominent of citizens—Haman! In a whirlwind of dust, she raced her chariot toward the palace. Though it was uncustomary and even perilous for anyone, including the queen, to go to the king unannounced, she had made up her mind. She was going to go see him first thing in the morning.

Moonbeams danced through the canopy of trees lining the palace drive. It was well after dark. Her mind raced as fast as the wheels of her chariot. *I need to gather my servants. If it pleases the king, I am going to throw a banquet for him and invite Haman too.* Wisdom told her a banquet would set the king in a good mood and be the perfect time and place to reveal the underhanded scheming of Haman. She would expose his lies.

She knew Haman to be a conniving man—the kind of man who manipulated truth with convincing charm. She was sure her husband had been taken in by his deceit.

Stepping out of the chariot, she loosened the veil and pulled it down to where it rested on her shoulders. Her beauty was undeniable, almost competing with the stars above. Her long, chocolate hair curled gracefully down and around her olive-skinned shoulders. The king had chosen her from her peasant Jewish roots because he, too, had been captured by her beauty. It poured forth from her insides and graced everything she did, every silent movement she made.

If I perish, I perish, she said to herself as she leaped from the chariot and made her way up the palace steps. No matter what it cost her, in the morning she would do the right thing. *Haman might be a prominent and powerful man, but I will not stand by and watch his deceitfulness unfold.* At the palace's top step, she paused and looked up into the stars. She was queen of this great land of Susa. But inside she felt like that orphaned Jewish girl of so long ago, someone small against a big world. She knew she couldn't do this without Jehovah God. He had plucked her from obscurity and placed her in the palace. He would have to help her.

Misty-eyed, she stared into the night sky. The faint sounds of her people wailing in the distance filtered across the dark horizon and up the palace steps. Their anguished cries pulled at her heart. A shimmering star in the night caught her attention. It was strong and brilliant, almost grandly alone against the darkness. She wiped the tear from her cheek and straightened herself. She knew her Hebrew name meant "star." *Jehovah God, be with me,* she prayed.

With a host of heavenly confidence shining inside her, she turned and disappeared into the palace gates. She would go to the king in the morning and make her petition.

* * *

Looking to pull a star from the deep, she combed the beach. Every time she visited her folks in Florida, she went to the beach to find peace of mind and maybe another starfish to add to her collection back home. Her two little girls scurried up the shoreline ahead of her.

"Mommy, we found one!" one of the girls squealed as she squeamishly picked the starfish up by one of its legs and placed it into the pail.

"Be sure to put some water in with it," she reminded them.

"Why?" came the childlike questioning.

"Because starfish can't live without being in water," she replied.

"Why?"

"Their legs will start to drop off if you don't put them in water."

"Why?"

"Because God made them so they would fight to survive, even if it means dropping a leg or two."

"It's better they live without a leg than die with all of them on?" one of the girls asked.

"Yup. Now let's keep looking for treasures." And with that, her two little girls bounded on up the beach looking to pull stars from the deep.

Meanwhile, her mind wandered back to her accounting firm. Part of the reason she had flown down to Florida was to get away from it all. Her husband had encouraged her to take a needed break and go see her folks. She didn't argue. The past several months had drained her physically, mentally, emotionally, and maybe even a little bit spiritually, if she dared admit it.

I'm so tired of being tired, Lord—tell me what to do, she prayed as she kept an eye on her daughters. She even prayed for the former colleagues who had sabotaged her accounting career. They had sucker-punched her but good. They had taken her career, her stock, and more damaging, they had tarnished her reputation with clients. That was something she wouldn't be able to rebuild overnight. She hoped there would be a few who would see through the slander and decide to stick with her as she started up her own accounting firm. She would find out who would be willing to do that when she got back from her trip.

For now, she combed the beach for washed-up starfish. *That's what I am*, she said to herself as she picked up a starfish from the shoreline. W*ho would follow a washed-up starfish? Probably no one.* She felt weak in the knees.

Despite her burdened heart, it was a beautiful day. The sun warmed her to the bone and deepened her tan. Walking along the beach quieted her soul in a way nothing else could. Here she could walk and pray and think things through. She loved her accounting career. She had worked hard to get to where she was. In just under 10 years, she had earned a senior partner position and accrued more than $200,000 worth of well-earned company stock.

But what meant more to her than anything was the reputation she had helped the company build. Both the employees and people in the community knew it to be a company they could trust. That was what she was most proud of.

Then, one Monday morning, everything changed. The

minute she walked through the front doors, she could sense something was wrong. The receptionist didn't give her typical grin and greeting but instead looked away and began busying herself with some typing. Young trainees filed awkwardly by her, dropping their glances to the floor. Her long-time colleagues sauntered by, studying their coffee cups. Others gave a shallow "How you doing?" It was as if some sort of edict had gone forth, and she was the only one who hadn't read it. In fact, that was exactly what had happened.

Before she had arrived at the office, a staff meeting had been called. Employees were informed of her termination before she was. She hadn't an inkling that they had even had a grievance! No one had approached her or met with her about anything nor given her the courtesy to explain her side of the situation. Where was the professionalism? Better yet, where was basic human dignity? Being forthcoming, she supposed, would have weakened their position and spoiled their plans for her swift removal.

The first move was to shift office opinion against her without her knowledge. The early-morning meeting they held with staff accomplished that. There they planted their clever half-truths. And it worked like a charm.

What in the world is going on? she thought as she set her purse down near her desk. With the twisted influence established in the office, they allowed her to hang her coat up before calling her into an urgent meeting. It was a surreal meeting. She sat for what seemed like hours across from her partners and listened in disbelief as they shared the trumped-up charges of her engaging in company misconduct. In disbelief, she said nothing.

After nearly 10 years of impeccable service and shared mentoring, mentoring that made them what *they* were, too—she couldn't believe her ears. All she could do was laugh inside. Yes, laugh. It was just that ridiculous. For a brief moment she didn't hear a word they were saying. It was as if God had descended on her heart and allowed her a glimpse of the spiritual battle taking place across the desk from her. Calmly, she folded one hand over the other and rubbed the starfish bracelet around her wrist.

This is a bigger battle than just an earthly one, isn't it, Lord? she prayed as she sat in disbelief and listened to her accusers continue their charges. Their voices grew muffled as if she were listening to them under water. Like the starfish on her bracelet, she was out of her comfort zone and could feel her legs drop out from beneath her. She wiped a tear from her cheek and tried straightening herself in the chair. Their accusations continued. She slid back down.

I am a competent C.P.A., she told herself. But in that moment at that office, she felt more like a little girl, someone small up against a big world. She couldn't find the floor with her feet. She gave up and slumped helplessly in her chair. There seemed to be no end to their accusations. It was as if they had never been partners. It was as if they had never been friends.

* * *

Feeling the sand between her toes, she strolled the beach and thought about her name. She had never much liked the meaning of her name. Tracey meant *fighter*. She certainly didn't consider herself to be much of a fighter. Truth be known, she had resigned herself to thinking it wasn't the Christian thing to do. *Fighter, me? Yeah, right.* But maybe that was just a nice excuse to do what her flesh felt comfortable doing, stepping to the side.

"Don't be afraid to get your feet wet!" she called up the beach to the girls, who were busy keeping themselves far from the ebb and flow of the shoreline. "You'll never find any treasures that way!" she hollered. The words had no more left her mouth when she felt the ping in her heart. She repented. *If you want me to jump in and fight this thing, God, I'll fight. If you want me to walk away, I'll walk away.*

Either way, she purposed in her heart that day that she would see the spiritual battle behind the earthly battle—it was a battle for their conniving hearts. *It probably put my family in financial straits to fight them in the courts, Lord. But I'm willing to trust that part to you, too.* Something other than her own comfort-seeking flesh told her that there *are* times when the principles of honesty and fairness are worth fighting for. And for such a time as this, she was called to fight that good fight. *If I perish, I perish,* she prayed aloud.

With that, she continued down the sunny beach with goose bumps still on her arms from His presence and a better understanding of what she was to do when she returned home. No matter how high the cost, she was going to stand up to those corporate bullies. Perhaps God had given her peace about confronting them, because He had seen she was willing to *not* stand up to them. Maybe that was it. She wasn't sure why it was to be played out this way—she just knew it was. Maybe it was to keep it from happening to the next person. Maybe it was to show her accusers they were accountable for their slanderous words and ultimately accountable to a higher being. She didn't know. She only knew she was surprised to find herself taking such a counterintuitive path. Would they see the heart of her God through her actions? She hoped so. She prayed so.

"Mommy!" called a voice.

"Yes, honey," she replied, retreating from her thoughts.

"We found a starfish without a leg! It's yucky!"

"It's not yucky—it's just fighting to survive," she heard herself say.

"God made it that way. Right, Mom?"

"Yup." she whispered. *OK, Lord—I hear you,* she prayed.

She knew the Lord was with her, that He was reminding her that she was His fighting star from the deep—created to shine in the darkness.

Peace flooded her little-girl fears.

As she and her daughters walked home with their treasures in tow, she smiled. This she knew for certain:

sometimes along the shores of Florida God pulls stars from the deep and helps them grow legs of strength for purposes bigger than themselves.

* * *

We all know the Hamans of life. Some of us, unfortunately, know them a little better than others. For whatever reason, misrepresentation is their tool of choice. They don't tell boldface lies. First, they distort the truth by planting empathetic seeds about themselves and how misunderstood they are. They are charming, half-truth-tellers. They slay a victim and then *play* the victim, and in the end they are able to curry favor with the masses and convince the most objective thinkers into believing that up is down and down is up. Hamans are charming masters of deceit. That's what makes them so formidable.

Like Haman in the Bible, they demand your respect and insist that you bow down to them. And if you won't, before you know it they'll have you by the hair dragging you down a slandering path in an attempt to destroy your credibility, possibly your career, and most certainly your reputation.

But that's not all. For an encore, you'll get to bear the brunt of glares from those whom they've convinced *you're* the big, bad wolf! You'll wonder why those glaring at you can't see the patches of hair missing from your scalp.

Whether you ever find yourself on such a circus ride or not, know this: Sometimes God will call you to confront

Haman. Sometimes not. But always He will call you to pray for Haman. And as hard as that is, you need to give him the one thing he has not yet taken from you—your prayers. By all means, pray for the truth to be revealed, for his unmerciful lies to be found out. But along with those prayers, also pray for God to bless Haman—yes, for God to bless him. For the battle Haman is engaged in is not just with you and your flesh but with another—that charming angel who parades himself as light—*the father of lies*. As hard as it is to watch your loved ones or yourself be slandered, there's more at stake than your and your family's reputation and credibility. Haman's credibility before God is on the line. His soul is in the balance. Pray that he can find his way out from his sticky webs of deceit before he ends up like Haman from the Bible, hanging from his own gallows.

At the Gallows

False accusations paraded as truth is a formidable enemy.
And so it was for our Lord.
Of the three nails that pierced Him,
surely misrepresentation was one of them.
A rope of twisted words upon a scaffold of half-truths
can hang the best of reputations.
In righteous anger one prays,

May they hang like Haman from the gallows
they've so skillfully prepared for another.

Poetic justice comforts as the heart envisions the slanderer
walking the scaffold to face his own noose of careless words.

And for a moment, the heart finds relief and even rejoices,
until dimly there is seen a figure that shocks and halts victory.

There, at the foot of the scaffold, the soul faints to bended knee as it horrifically discovers it has marched to the gallows of not just its offender—but the One willing to take both their places. The sway of *His* silhouette brushes the soul's battered cheek and the tear shed in anger now falls in shame.

The gavel of poetic justice forever lassoed by
Christ's swaying lyric of love.

—Jody

4
SILENT NIGHT

FACING LIMITED RESOURCES

The Shepherd who found this lost life of mine has since asked of me one thing: that I lose it.
—Jody

A GENTLE SNOW clipped the row of windows nestled below the four-story orphanage. It was late or early morning, depending on one's point of view. The children were all fast asleep in their bunks. The glow of a single kerosene lantern meandered from bed to bed. Occasionally the soft glow paused to tuck in a loose arm or leg.

The orphanage's large upstairs room was spacious and housed 22 bunks, and except for the drafts that swept across the hardwood floors, it was a perfect room for the children. Tonight, however, it was especially chilly even for Bristol, England's, winter months. Donated quilts from last year's Christmas party draped the bunks—every bunk except for little Maggie's. She had just arrived at Ashley Downs. Tattered edges and loose strands hung from her worn and thinning blanket.

The heavy blanket brought up from downstairs was quickly unfolded and so carefully laid into the place of the worn one that little Maggie barely stirred. *She'll sleep more soundly now,* he thought. With Maggie's tattered old blanket now draped in his arms, Mr. Mueller picked up his lantern and made his way down to the second-floor landing. It would be daylight in a few hours. He best keep his appointment if he were to feed the children by six.

The wooden floors captured the soft glow of the lantern and illuminated each step of the narrow and winding staircase. Twisting and untwisting one of the loose strands from Maggie's worn blanket around his index finger, he continued down the staircase to a long hallway that led to his private quarters. *I have only a few hours left*, he thought as he entered his bedroom. Draping the blanket over a chair, he set the lantern on the nightstand. With one of the loose strands from Maggie's blanket still tied around his finger, he stumbled through the dimly lit room to his closet. Turning the knob, he slipped inside.

Daybreak came quickly. The morning sun streamed through the frosty fourth-floor windows, stirring the occupant of each bunk awake. Maggie pulled her knees to her chest and slumbered a few more minutes under her toasty new blanket. Soon hunger pains set her straight up in bed. She rubbed her eyes, blinked a bit, and greeted the day with her usual smile.

"Good morning!" she chirped to the others still nestled under their covers. Swinging her feet over the side of her bunk, she wrapped her new blanket around her shoulders and bounded toward the windows.

"It snowed—it snowed, everyone!" she exclaimed with her nose pressed against the frosted pane. The other boys and girls soon stirred enough to climb down out of their bunks. Sleepy-eyed, they filed by her, yawning their way down the stairs to the main floor. Maggie slipped on down ahead. She couldn't wait to tell Mr. Mueller about the blanket of snow outside her window.

"Where's Mr. Mueller, Miss Nance?" Maggie asked with a hop.

"Haven't seen him yet this morning, little Mags," replied Miss Nance, who was busy setting two long farmhouse tables with 43 plates and cups. Miss Nance was the house servant. She wore a white cap that kept her hair up and a long, white apron around her waist. She usually hummed while she set the table. It was nice, and this morning was no different.

Mr. Mueller suddenly appeared from around the corner of the dining room.

"Mr. Mueller, Mr. Mueller—isn't it wonderful? It snowed! It snowed!" Maggie ran and jumped into his outstretched arms.

"You don't say," replied Mr. Mueller with a tug on her nose. "Well, this morning is a morning for wonderful possibilities." Miss Nance continued setting the table but stopped humming long enough to give Mr. Mueller a worried look.

The pantry at Ashley Downs was running low on supplies—not just on a few supplies but on all supplies. It was essentially bare. Miss Nance wasn't sure what she was going to feed the children this morning. She stood staring at the long tables now set with empty plates and mugs. Things looked bleak for the children at George Mueller's orphanage. It was time for breakfast, and there was no food—not a crumb.

Miss Nance looked again to Mr. Mueller for some sort of reassurance. His gaze was waiting for hers. He smiled as if he knew something she didn't and then swung little Maggie around in his arms.

"It's a morning for wonderful possibilities, right, little Mags?" he said through her giggles. Meanwhile, the other children sleepily filed to the breakfast table and took their seats.

"Come. Let's see what our Father will do, little Maggie." And with that, Mr. Mueller took her by the hand and led her to the breakfast table where the other children were seated. At the head of two farm tables full of hungry faces and empty plates, Mr. Muller took his seat and bowed his head.

"Dear Father, we thank Thee for what Thou art going to give us to eat." Within minutes there came a knock at the door. "I'll get it," piped each of the children.

"Stay in your seats," ordered Miss Nance as she pushed her chair back from the table and bustled herself to the front door. A moment later, she returned to the dining room with the local baker by her side.

"Mr. Muller," said the baker cupping and turning his hat in his hands. "I couldn't sleep a wink last night. Somehow, I felt—why, I felt like you might need some bread down here, so I got me-self up at two o'clock this 'ere morning and baked some loaves of fresh bread. I don't know what got into me. Anyway, the baskets are just inside the door."

Mr. Mueller thanked him, and out the door he went as quickly as he had come. Miss Nance set the baskets of warm bread on the table and went to the kitchen to retrieve some homemade jam and butter. Jam and butter were about the only things left in the Ashley Downs kitchen. Miss Nance kept some jam in the freezer from the batch she had made last summer.

No sooner had she returned with the butter and jam then did there come a second knock on the door. The hungry children were too busy passing around the baskets of warm bread to notice. Soon Miss Nance appeared from around the corner with a wire basket holding four bottles of fresh milk.

"Anyone for milk?" she bubbled, trying to contain her enthusiasm. Making her way around the tables, she hummed and poured each cup to the rim as she explained to everyone how the milkman had just finished his morning deliveries when his cart broke down up the street. "There were only a few bottles left from his rounds," she explained, "and he wondered if we couldn't just take the last remaining milk off his hands so he could go get his cart fixed!"

As Miss Nance bustled around the tables humming and refilling cups, Mr. Mueller watched each hungry orphan eat his or her fill. Twisting and untwisting the string from his finger, he relived the hours just before daybreak. It *had* been a morning of wonderful possibilities. His closet petitions had been answered.

"It snowed, Mr. Mueller! It snowed!" Maggie reminded him as she chomped on a mouthful of food.

"Indeed it did!" he smiled.

In the upper corners of her milk-frosted grin, he could sense the same shadowing presence from his closet. Over those 43 orphans stood the presence of a Silent Knight. Mr. Mueller knew who it was who was watching over them.

"Thank you," he said aloud.

* * *

Another morning of manna? She grumbled to herself as she flapped the opening of the tent back and stomped out into the morning light. Squinting around, she could see that most of the Israelite camp was already out scavenging the ground like grouse. She guessed she had better get to scooping up the pearly white barley heads before the stuff started melting. *We ate better in Egypt as slaves.* Disgruntled, she continued scooping the manna into her wooden bowl. She would eat breakfast on the go this morning—that way she wouldn't have to visit with any of the others in camp. *I wonder if that Moses really knows what he's doing.*

Shoveling the last bite into her mouth, she tossed the empt bowl back inside. *Miriam would know,* she said to herself. She had thought twice about leaving a little in her bowl for a mid-morning snack, but one of her Israelite friends had tried that and said that it had turned mealy before she could eat it for a snack! *Yuck! I don't want to be sleeping with meal worms tonight.* With disgust, she secured the flap of her tent. *And to think that Moses wants to save an omer of this stuff to show to future generations!*

"What a legacy!" she grumbled aloud as she slipped into her sandals. It was time to find Miriam. She was probably down by the water. It was too bitter to drink, but one could at least stick her feet in it on a hot day. Today looked like another hot day in the desert sands, a perfect day to dip one's feet and do some visiting. Maybe Miriam could get her brother to do something about the lack of pretty much everything in this camp.

* * *

God's provision is a funny thing. It's not that God doesn't do His part and provide. It's that sometimes it's all in the eye of the beholder. While some grumble about the humble manna in front of them, others can look at the same humble scraps and see the hand of God in them and give thanks. George Mueller fed and built housing for tens of thousands of orphans and didn't have a dime to do it. He funded it all on his knees.

Every time the "thorn of lack" tried to buckle him and chide him into a panic about his orphans' insurmountable needs, he hit his knees. From just after midnight until morning, he went to his prayer closet and talked things over with his Heavenly Father. His prayer closet was where he did business. It's where he bathed the needs of his heart, the needs of his house. It's where God met him and helped him feed and clothe thousands upon thousands of orphans. While he passed from this world having left—by worldly standards—a beggar's bank account, his legacy is one of the richest in all of England's history.

Mr. Mueller knew what the apostle Paul meant when he said he had learned to be content in need and in plenty. He knew that the thorn in his side could bring about Kingdom purposes. Whether there's "fruit on the vine or not," Mr. Mueller's heart—his Habakkuk heart—led him to set the table anyway and sit down and give thanks. The Habakkuk heart gives thanks that God is God whether the plate is full or not. It gives thanks whether what's on the plate is pleasing or not. The Habakkuk heart gives thanks because ultimately it is a heart that trusts that what is provided or not provided will shape and serve Kingdom purposes.

Are you down to the last crumbs? Physically? Mentally? Emotionally? Spiritually? Is there nothing, not even an omer of hope to draw from? Maybe you're doing all you can to provide for your family, and yet you find yourself still living hand to fist on many levels of life. You have two choices. You can find a friend and go sit beside bitter waters and grumble, or you can bind the hope of Resurrection Sunday around your heart and mind and life and head to your prayer closet and petition your Heavenly Father. He's there waiting. He'll give you the strength you need to bow before an empty plate and give thanks.

Maybe He will provide you with your request, and maybe He won't. Give thanks anyway—not because God is a cosmic vending machine and will plop something into your lap. No, give thanks because you were able to walk to the table on healthy legs. Give thanks that your family made it home safely and is around that table. Give thanks that you have been placed in their lives and are able to put smiles on their faces in a way no one else can.

Yes, before an empty plate give thanks. Then step back and watch what happens. Your needs will be met in ways you never thought possible. Moreover, you'll sense the presence of that same shadowing presence from your prayer closet. It's the Silent Knight. And He stands ready to take your late-night petitions and fill your morning plate with surpassing peace.

Silent Night

In a dry dandelion's bouquet of bursting seed,
In the formation of birds flying in perfect symphony
The Night of Silence speaks.

In the bloom of a rose,
In a rainbow's brushstroke
The Night of Silence speaks.

In a blanketed countryside of snow,
In the spawning of salmon undertow,
The Night of Silence speaks.

In the ballet of butterflies across open meadows,
In the waltz of a horse's mane with the wind,
In the synchronized dance of planetary giants,
In the sun's exit of siren red
The Night of Silence speaks.

But never has silence so eloquently spoken
than on that night long ago
when God allowed man to swaddle Him.
The Knight of Silence speaks!

—Jody

5
AN ALABASTER JAR

FACING THE LOSS OF A CHILD

*Allow God to take life's broken shards
and knit them into a stained-glass mosaic
through which those inside the church and those
outside the church will be compelled to peer.*

—Jody

AN UPSTAIRS NURSERY WINDOW framed the horizon's rolling farmland. Cutting through the picturesque landscape, predictable fence posts escorted a dusty lane past waving grain now crowding to the edge of the roadway. It was harvest time. Each farm dotting the rolling hills nudged the dawn, eager to get a start on the day's preparations.

Meanwhile, in the upstairs nursery, preparations of a different sort were being made. An oversized window seat cushion with Mother Goose print sat hushing the colorful picture books on its built-in shelf below. The surrounding baby-blue walls whispered their excitement while the animated crib sheets chatted enthusiastically with the mobile of bucking horses circling joyfully overhead. Nearby, stacked diapers boldly told their stories to a crowd of teddy bears dressed in their Sunday-best bows. But it was the tiny, hooded robe patiently hanging in the corner that gave the most eloquent testimony of all. Indeed, a most important life was on the way.

Then . . .

The ringing of the phone eerily interrupted as if to warn of an approaching hailstorm. The words hit hard. Fencerows seemed to snap in two as farm after farm learned the unbearable news of the young couple's newborn baby being airlifted to a major medical center. The barbed information swiftly snagged the tidy yolk of seasons, severing the sacred trust between seedtime and harvest, between sowing and reaping, leaving a labor cheated of its fruit.

Upon a hospital's treadmill of endless hallways, a vigorous marathon of pacing, praying, and hoping began and never ended until three days later, when an exhausted young couple would ask family and friends to gather round. In a small hospital room they would rock their son, Thomson, for the first and last time. In a silent, tearful dance, family and friends encircled the couple, stepping forward one at a time to caress the first-time parents as they rocked and kissed their precious baby boy hello and goodbye.

The Father's Day holiday traffic pummeled the young couple all the long ride home. Back at the farm, the upstairs nursery sat quietly. The oversized Mother Goose cushion on the new built-in window seat had no one to hush. The baby-blue walls were—just that. The mobile of horses hung motionless. The crowd of wide-eyed teddy bears were not so wide-eyed. And the tiny hooded robe patiently hanging in the corner had grown impatient.

Outside the window the dusty lane seemed more crooked than before. And though robust fields applauded the coming of harvest, in the heart of a small farming community the unthinkable had happened.

Later, in one blurry and surreal blink, a first-time mom found herself in front of a packed congregation cradling nothing but a children's book. With tears rolling down her cheeks, she began to read. Her soft voice seemed to transport an entire congregation into an imaginary nursery room. No one stirred. From the pages of a picture book, a young mother gave shadow to the baby she would never bring home.

Before returning to her seat, she said, "I watched my precious son suffer. And no matter what I did, I couldn't stop it. I couldn't stop him from dying. And it amazes me to think that God watched His precious Son suffer. And He could have stopped it, but He didn't. He didn't because He loved me."

Her composure had given her husband the added strength he needed to address the congregation. He stood. The three broad steps encasing the platform loomed ahead of him like an impossible mountain. But he was sure of God's Word. With a deep sigh, he climbed the steps to the pulpit. It was a ledge unlike any he had ever climbed before. Something inside him told him it was the kind of ledge only the most faithful climb. Each cascading step to the pulpit seemed to tauntingly say, *So this God of yours would have you give up your son? Remember when you first heard his little heartbeat, when you first laid eyes on his tussle of black hair? Remember when you first held his tiny hand in yours? And now this? What kind of God is worth all of this?*

His footing felt uneasy. It wasn't that he doubted God. It was just that he found himself between two loves, between two loyalties. He was suspended between his Almighty Creator and his precious son.

At the pulpit of the God he loved, his waging heart gave tribute not only to his son lying in the casket before him but also to his God above. He would have given anything to have just taken his son home. But it was not to have been. Before turning to leave, he asked a tearful congregation if they wouldn't please stop and look, though difficult, at the pictures of the son of whom he was so very proud.

Wearily he added, "Thomson touched so many people in his brief life, and if he causes one person to think about eternity, if his life causes one person to trust in Jesus Christ as his or her personal Savior, then I would do it all again in a heartbeat.

* * *

Now it came about after these things, that God tested Abraham, and said to him, "Abraham!" and he said, "Here I am." He said, "Take now your son, your only son, whom you love, Isaac, and go to the land of Moriah, and offer him there as a burnt offering on one of the mountains of which I will tell you." So Abraham rose early in the morning and saddled his donkey, and took two of his young men with him and Isaac his son *(Gen. 22:1-3).*

The broad foothills encasing Moriah loomed ahead of Abraham like an impossible mountain. But he was sure of God's Word. With a deep sigh, he began making the necessary preparations to give up his treasure—his son. He began splitting wood. Each hesitating swing gave a haunting preview of what was to come. The foothills around him seemed to stand on tiptoe as if to sneak a peek at the sorrow that was sure to unfold later that day. At the height of every chop, the axe head seemed to mock the stars that hid within them a cherished oath. Swiftly it lowered its hollow chunk against the firewood, practicing its role of splintering God's promise of descendants.

The woodchips around his worn sandals seemed to tauntingly say, *So this God of yours would have you give up your son? Remember when you rocked Isaac under the desert sky, when you ran to rescue him the day he ventured too far over the sandy dunes? Remember when you sat up all night watching the horizon for his familiar gait as he strolled in from the flock? And now this? What kind of God is worth all this?*

Abraham shook the taunting woodchips from his sandals and said to his young men, "Stay here with the donkey, and I and the lad will go over there; and we will worship and return to you" (v. 5). Up a winding ledge he and Isaac climbed. It was a ledge unlike any he had ever climbed. Something inside him told him it was the kind of ledge only the most faithful climb. The closer to the top he got, the more uneasy his footing felt. It wasn't that he doubted God. It was just that he found himself between two loves, between two loyalties, suspended between his Almighty Creator and his precious son.

> So, the two of them walked on together. Then they came to the place of which God had told him; and Abraham built the altar there and arranged the wood, and bound his son Isaac and laid him on the altar, on top of the wood *(Gen. 22:8-9)*.

With a warring heart, he gently covered his boy's eyes and said his goodbyes. He would have given anything to have simply taken Isaac home. But it was not to be. With the other hand, "Abraham stretched out his hand and took the knife to slay his son" (Gen. 22:10)—but not before a lifetime of memories flashed before him.

When it came to working with his son, he wasn't sure where the sweat of his own brow ended and where his son's began. Whether digging the family well or sheering the flock, he and Isaac worked as one. In the early part of the week they went out and marked off pasture for the family livestock. In the evenings they made working ropes. Occasionally they stopped to delight in the work of their hands in each intricately woven rope.

Smiling, Abraham remembered how they had both gone out and provided for the family. Against the morning's crisp skyline, they raised their bows and in perfect sync released their arrows. He marveled at Isaac's marksmanship. There were other memories, too, memories of how they had surprised Sarah with a bouquet of desert blooms and how their laughter filled the canyons as they pitched the family tent.

All these memories echoed up through the outstretched knife. But before its shiny blade could mock the stars that hid within them a cherished oath, heaven saw the steadfast stance of Abraham's heart. And heaven recoiled, shouting, "Abraham, Abraham! . . . Do not stretch out your hand against the lad, and do nothing to him; for now I know that you fear God, since you have not withheld your son, your only son, from Me. Then Abraham raised his eyes and looked, and behold, behind him a ram caught in the thicket by his horns; and Abraham went and took the ram and offered him up for a burnt offering in the place of his son" (Gen. 22:11-13).

There was, to Abraham's great relief, a ram in the thicket. No longer would he need to sacrifice his precious son Isaac, the son with whom he had walked through life, the son whose companion prints crisscrossed with his own through the desert sands. No longer must he sacrifice the very one who had wound the string around the altar's bundled firewood.

The God Abraham loved had provided. But what God did for Abraham He did not do for himself. In the dawn of time, the hillsides encasing Golgotha loomed ahead of our Heavenly Father. It was a ledge unlike any other. It was a ledge only the most faithful climb. So up He went. The closer He got to the top, the more uneasy his footing felt. It wasn't that He doubted His master plan. It was just that He found himself between two loyalties, between two loves, suspended between His only begotten Son and the world He so loved.

Each cascading step toward Golgotha's altar seemed to tauntingly say, *Remember when you built the storehouses of snow together and wound the rings around the sequoias? Remember when you and your Son crisscrossed the earth, leaving companion prints to form its lakes? Remember when you both designed the bumblebee and then trained its pudgy frame to fly? And now this? Is humanity really worth all this?* He would have given anything simply to take his Son home that Friday.

With each step, a lifetime of infinite memories flashed before Him. When it came to working with His Son, He wasn't sure where the sweat of His brow had ended and where His Son's had begun. Whether sheering the snowcap of the mountains or collecting the morning dew, they had worked as One. In the beginning, they had gone out and marked off the foundations of the world. Then they had braided ropes of DNA. Occasionally, they had stopped and delighted in the work of their hands, in each intricately woven individual

Smiling, the Heavenly Father remembered how they had gone out together and provided for Noah's family. Against the morning's crisp skyline, they had raised their rainbow, promising to never again flood the earth. And then, in perfect sync, they had released from their crossbow Calvary's arrow, which would shoot through time and fulfill the promise of redemption for the family of humanity. There were other memories too, memories of the day they had dug the recesses of the deep, the night they had spent laughing as they pitched a canopy of stars, and the time they had sketched a smile upon the moon.

Then the mallet lowered. The steely sound of its chunking against the six-inch nails mocked the heavens, seemingly shattering the hope of salvation. No voice from heaven sent reprieve. No ram rustled Calvary's thicket. No intervention was made. Only the voices of both the mockers who spat upon Him and the soldiers who gambled for His garments could be heard.

The Heavenly Father watched it all, every heartbreaking moment. He watched His Son suffer and die. He could have stopped it, but He didn't. He didn't—because He so loved the world.

* * *

Some have been fortunate enough to have had a ram rustle the thicket in a time of need. Some have had prayers miraculously answered. How wonderful! But for others, the thicket stands empty. For some, life resembles a broken alabaster jar. One minute life is perfect, and the next minute it lies before them in pieces. If you are one who can't seem to find hope, if no matter how hard you try you can't piece your life back together, if despite prayer you hear no rustling in the thicket, go like that young couple to the altar. Though your heart wages war, climb the steep ledge of the faithful. The Almighty will meet you there with His alabaster jar.

There you will find a Father who not only promises to be with you but who has also walked in advance the valley you now face. He's stood where you are. And He'll wrap your seemingly unanswered prayers in the blessed knowledge that He, too, faced an empty thicket. He'll wipe away your tears and help you place your brokenness inside His once-broken alabaster jar, wherein at your fingertips the promise of your resurrected life in His resurrected life can be realized—and wherein you'll discover that God will never call you into a valley He hasn't already kneeled in himself. In His resurrection scars you'll find a peace, a hope, and a future that will not disappoint.

Before you turn to leave your broken heart at the altar of your Heavenly Father, He'll share with you how very proud He is of His Son, and He may even ask if you wouldn't please stop, though difficult, and picture His Son on the Cross. Through gentle tears you'll hear Him say, "For you I'd do it all again in a heartbeat."

6
BROKEN FOR VOWS

FACING INJURY IN THE LINE OF DUTY

In the sin of another I see my own;
for us both I go to the Father's throne.
Quarry in these hearts of stone;
a righteousness be pleased to hone.
—Jody

STOREFRONT AWNINGS FLAPPED in the gentle breeze, waving to the bumper-to-bumper traffic making its way through town to the college campus some 20 miles south. It was game day. Traffic had slowed to a crawl. The quaint shops along the bottlenecked street proudly sported their neighboring college colors, but not without also beckoning travelers to stop and enjoy "The Best Burgers in the World" at the 50s-style malt shop or enticing travelers to find that one-of-a-kind treasure at the antique shop on the corner.

It was September.

"Steptoe, Paul 32, in service," relayed Deputy McMurray over his patrol car radio. He was just starting his shift, and like all deputies working that weekend, Deputy McMurray knew the top priority for the day was traffic safety. Hundreds upon hundreds of fans would be hitting the roads, driving everything from motorcycles to motor homes, and it was a certainty that for many, alcohol would be a traveling companion.

Boy, it's muggy today! he thought as he slid into the seat of his cruiser. The black interior always baked in the sun. He could feel the sweat bead down his back beneath his standard-issue bulletproof vest as he leaned forward to hang the radio mic back on the dashboard hook. As a deputy *and* the county chaplain, he had taken an oath to serve and protect the many communities that dotted the county.

He enjoyed the blending of the two jobs. After several years of service, there was one aspect to them, however, that he never quite got used to—notifying families of their loved one's life-threatening injury or of the person's death. It wasn't that he was awkward at it; he actually handled it well. He had a gift of compassion and a discernment that told him when an empathizing presence spoke more than any word could. It was a delicate kind of work, the kind that rendered an officer's vest and Glock useless. The chaplain in him required a different kind of sidearm—the Holy Spirit.

May I be sensitive to your leading today. Checking his review mirrors, he pulled his cruiser from the parking space and began his shift for that afternoon. With him went the code, the unspoken commitment officers pledged to one another. That code weaves stability through the brotherhood. It's what keeps every officer doing his or her utmost, knowing that should trouble arise, other units will race to the destination in a matter of minutes. They have each other's backs. Deputy McMurray entered the flow of traffic with that promise. He would be on duty only a few hours before he would need that promise as never before.

"We have a hit-and-run in progress," reported the county dispatcher. "Apparently a driver has rammed their vehicle into the side of one of the parked patrol cars behind the sheriff's office and is now attempting to elude."

Who would want to hit a parked police car? He flipped his cruiser around and sped back toward the sheriff's office. The radio traffic was full of responding officers relaying their failing attempts to stop the now-eluding vehicle. Behind the professional calm of each transmission, he sensed the grave concern as the vehicle entered the congested roadways full of weekend football fans. The attempts of both local and county officers were proving fruitless.

It didn't take long to figure out that this driver was on a mission and bent on destruction. The reckless chase that had begun behind the sheriff's office wove through side streets onto Main Street and was now in the main artery of heavy traffic, Highway 95. With other officers already engaged in the pursuit, Officer McMurray was instructed to head back to the sheriff's office and retrieve spike strips for a possible roadblock.

He was halfway there already. Back at the office, he grabbed the spike strips and jumped back into his cruiser. He would have to hurry if he was going to catch up with his fellow officers who were chasing the northbound vehicle toward the county line.

"Use extreme caution—suspect is weaving through traffic and topping speeds of 100," he heard the dispatcher report as he peeled away from the curb with the spike strips in tow.

The guys are counting on these spike strips. Within minutes he was in the thick of traffic on 95. Except for a few corners, it was basically 60 miles of straight highway that ran smack through the middle of rolling farmland hills.

Like a salmon swimming against the current, he cautiously sped, lights and sirens blaring, in and around motorists, sling-shotting past traffic as safely as possible. "The suspect is a woman and has now flipped a U-turn and is heading back south on Highway 95," radioed the dispatcher. "I repeat, the eluding woman driver is now southbound."

What in the world? Deputy McMurray continued listening to the radio traffic as he sped to where the roadblock was to be set up. "Also," the dispatcher continued, "the eluding driver seems to be playing chicken with oncoming traffic and has forced a semi-truck off the roadway."

The sunny day matched the faces of the unsuspecting motorists. They grinned with pre-game euphoria, utterly unaware of the reckless driver bulleting up and down their stretch of road playing Russian roulette with their lives.

I've got to get these people off the roadways. She's coming our way. The roadblock was to be set up at milepost 56. He could see it up ahead and was almost there. Pursuing officers would be coming from the opposite direction in pursuit of the southbound vehicle. According to radio traffic, they would reach milepost 56 within minutes.

He came to a quick stop, threw the cruiser into park, popped the trunk, and ran back to where the traffic was beginning to pile up behind his bumper. He ordered all immediate vehicles and their passengers to pull as far off onto the shoulder of the roadway as they could get. "We have a car that will be barreling down on top of us in a matter of minutes!" he shouted. "You people need to get into the fields where it's safe!" he ordered as he ran to each rig, warning them of the impending danger.

Like mice scurrying into nearby fields, not exactly

sure what they were taking refuge from, the motorists chattered up the roadside bands, climbing through the field stubble to the top of the hill. Against the pristine blue sky they stood, out of breath and wondering what could be so pressing as to interrupt their day. With curiosity, they gazed out over the highway below them and watched in true spectator fashion.

Deputy McMurray coached each motorist to climb farther up the hillside before he ran back to his cruiser and retrieved the gridiron of spike strips from the trunk. Within seconds the metal strip was perfectly deployed, cascading across the highway into perfect position—and not a moment too soon. In the distance, the sound of sirens blared. Then a vehicle screamed into sight. Like billiard balls in a game of pool, the eluding vehicle ricocheted around the corner and then seemed to shoot purposely into the oncoming lane, eight-balling fiercely toward the very police cruiser behind which Deputy McMurray had just taken cover. The crowds of people standing safely in the fields gasped as they braced for the inevitable high-speed impact.

It was forceful.

Deputy McMurray flew out of his boots and was propelled some 80 feet over the highway's guardrail. Flinging through the air, he landed head first at the bottom of a steep ravine. He laid stunned and unable to move. He couldn't breathe. He couldn't move. Like a rag doll, he lay at the bottom of a weedy roadside ravine. At first he wasn't quite sure what had hit him.

Disoriented, he lifted his head. *Where am I?* Peering down his chest, he surveyed the damage. His head throbbed. His ribs burned. Slowly, he reached up and felt the road rash and lacerations across his face. He wasn't sure where the blood was coming from, but it dripped down across his eyes. He hurt everywhere. But nothing compared to the pain from his left leg. He wondered if it was still there. He surveyed further.

Twisting off to one side in a contorted position, he could see a bone sticking through his bloodied pant leg. He felt woozy. The sharp pain took his breath away. Queasy and lightheaded, he let out a moan and rested his head back into the tall bramble brush. The weeds swallowed him. He wasn't sure which way was up. A sliver of blue sky seemed a million miles away. Turning his head toward it, he peered through the tall grass, knowing help would come. Soon he could make out two fuzzy figures climbing down the bank, making their way through the untamed brush toward him. They were shouting something. He couldn't make out their words. His head felt like it was slipping under water.

"Get a stretcher down here!" they yelled up the bank to the band of rescue units arriving on the scene. "Officer down!" Within moments he could feel the jarring of his body. He was being hoisted out of the deep ravine.

* * *

In a hospital waiting room, family and friends gathered and waited for minute-by-minute updates. All they knew for sure was that it wasn't good. Deputy McMurray's injuries were life-threatening. It was a wonder he was alive. But he was. All family and friends could do was wait and hope that he would pull through.

Time slowed. Time halted. Some in the waiting room sat with blank stares looking at the television bolted near the ceiling in the corner of the room. Others mindlessly thumbed through puzzle pieces laid out on a card table. Uniformed officers paced the halls with coffee in hand. Everyone waited for word. They paced and waited and thought about how preventable it all was.

How could someone have been so needlessly reckless? If she wanted to hurt herself, fine, but why hurt others? How could she have been so blatantly cruel? Such were the pacing thoughts of those sipping coffee and thumbing through the waiting room periodicals. Pacing thoughts gave way to anxious thoughts, which gave way to angry thoughts. It was the perfect temperature for bitterness to breed and anger to slow cook. If Deputy McMurray's offender had walked by that room at that time, there might have been an ugly scene. She had needlessly injured their loved one. For all they knew, she had taken his life.

Then came word from the emergency room chaplain. The entire room closed in around him as he took a seat. He had been able to speak with Deputy McMurray right before he was whisked away to emergency surgery.

"He's been severely hurt but is coherent," the chaplain explained. The room let out a collective sigh—he was alive.

"Your friend," he continued "must have a good sense of humor, because he managed to make a couple of jokes before going to surgery." Everyone smiled. That was the good-humored deputy they all knew and loved.

But it was what the chaplain said next that arrested every heart in the waiting room. Apparently, while Deputy McMurray was lying in the emergency room with broken ribs, road rash across his face, and a dangerous compound fracture of his left leg, he had asked, "How's she doing?"

Up until then, no one in the waiting room had cared enough to ask about her. But Deputy McMurray did.

* * *

A man was going down from Jerusalem to Jericho, and fell among robbers, and they stripped him and beat him, and went away leaving him half dead. And by chance a priest was going down on that road, and when he saw him, he passed by on the other side. Likewise a Levite also, when he came to the place and saw him, passed by on the other side. But a Samaritan, who was on a journey, came upon him; and when he saw him, he felt compassion, and came to him and bandaged up his wounds, pouring oil and wine on them; and he put him on his own beast, and brought him to an inn and took care of him. On the next day he took out two denarii and gave them to the innkeeper and said, "Take care of him; and whatever more you spend, when I return I will repay you" *(Luke 10:30-35)*.

* * *

Only the Habakkuk heart would care enough to ask about the one who had just steamrolled him. Like the Good Samaritan who bandaged the wounds of a known enemy, Deputy McMurray had poured oil into the life of his offender with those three little words and humbled an entire waiting room. "How's she doing?" As he lay broken and bleeding, his concern was not for himself and his life-threatening injuries but for a mixed-up woman. His thoughts were for his abuser.

When Goliath doesn't fall, a believer comes face-to-face with the Cross and gets a front-row seat with the Savior who went willingly. It's at the Cross that Christ was broken for His vows to protect humanity. While he was bleeding from a crown of thorns and the six-inch nails in His hands, His thoughts were not for himself but for His abusers. That's right—His thoughts were for those who had beaten Him, for those who had spat upon Him, for those who gambled for His garments.

"Father, forgive them." With those three words He poured oil into the life of all of us offenders. And that view gives grace-filled hope to us.

Milepost 56 isn't a place where a chaplain full of faith was miraculously delivered up from an unjust circumstance. It isn't a place where Goliath was made to swerve and miss. It is a place where not even the impact of a sadistic driver barreling down the highway at a deadly speed could knock the worship out of the Habakkuk heart. For the Habakkuk heart is anchored to a grace-filled foundation not of this world.

7
AN ALTAR FOR THE DEEP

FACING TERROR

When injustice tempts my heart to storm,
O Lord, keep the waters calm,
so that I might find my bearings
in the power of Your still reflection.
—Jody

IT WASN'T TOO LONG before the service was taxing the attention span of my three-year-old. It was time to duck out from the morning meeting at our church retreat. He put his little hand in mine, and we headed down to the swimming area. With a bagful of sand toys and plenty of snacks, we would be set for the next hour or so. The warm sand felt good between our toes. It was a perfect day. The sun glistened on the water, and a gentle breeze swept along the lakeshore.

As my son toddled back and forth, picking up rocks, I smiled at his cute little frame. One by one, he came and placed into my hand a rock he had found. By the end of the hour, I had more treasure than a king.

But there was one treasure that rarely left his pudgy grip. It was a tiny, yellow, plastic motorcycle he had retrieved from our beach bag. It was the kind of treasure no boy could share. I could have the rocks.

As he walked along, he occassionally stopped and squatted in the sand for a closer inspection of another pebble. He set his motorcycle down for only a moment. Suddenly, out of nowhere came a seagull. Swooping down, it snatched that toy from the sand. We blinked in disbelief. I knew seagulls were scavengers, but I had never seen one terrorize the skies like this and come in close enough to steal a toy motorcycle, of all things.

The look on my son's face was shock, as was mine. All we could do was watch that silly bird fly off into the blue yonder with that toy in its beak. With a worried look on his face and his little finger pointing toward the sky, he repeated over and over again, "Toi, bir. Toi, bir." Then he would look back at me for help. For the first time in his life, something he loved had been stolen from him.

Do you remember when you learned that this world would take something from you without batting an eye? Where were you when someone flat-out stole something from you? Maybe it was something material, or maybe it was your reputation. Maybe it was a lifelong dream. Do you remember standing there as pieces of you were carted off—stolen? The heart has a hard time healing from that kind of assault. For some, that reality has yet to touch their charmed lives. For most, it's a reality that tests one's faith to the limits.

A teenager now, my son laughs about that incident. Every time we see a seagull, we say, "I wonder if that's Steve." I don't know why we called that thieving bird "Steve," but we did. We should have named him something like "Harley."

To this day, we still comb the sand and pick up rocks on our camping trips. My son likes to run them through his rock tumbler. They come out looking like gems. The grinding from the tumbler makes every unique banding and fleck shine to a high gloss. Running them through the tumbler is the only way to bring out their beauty.

* * *

Squatting down in the dry riverbed for a closer inspection, the 12 men looked for a perfect rock. They were to carry out twelve rocks—one per man. *I can't believe I'm standing on dry ground,* they each thought as they stood up from their searching and looked around them. They were standing in the deepest part of Jordan's riverbed. The river's edge was several feet above their heads. They had walked down a slope to get to where they were standing. On one side of the riverbed an entire nation sat and waited and watched. On the other side of the river bed was Jericho.

The sound of water back-flushing from upstream seemed surreal. Where they stood there was normally 12 feet of water. They couldn't believe it, and they lingered in a gaze before continuing again with their combing of the strange moon-like surface. As each man found a rock, he made his way up the slope and out of the riverbed onto the other side. They all made their way carefully. A few unlucky fish, outwitted by the parting waters, squirmed among the rocks. They clutched their chosen rocks firmly. It was hard to believe the rocks they carried had only an hour earlier been submerged in several feet of rushing water.

"Over here, men!" shouted Joshua as he pointed to a tree just feet from the river's edge. "We'll make the altar here where our families will be camping tonight. That way, every time they see it, they'll remember how God helped them cross the Jordan on dry ground." As the men stacked their rocks and formed an altar beneath the tree, Joshua headed back to the middle of the dry riverbed where the priests stood with the Ark of the Covenant. At their feet, he gathered another 12 rocks and arranged them: an altar in the deep.

Afterward, 40,000 men dressed for battle walked by that altar with thousands of women and children behind them. As they descended into the deep riverbed, they were reminded that they weren't alone after all—God was with them.

* * *

"What?" he said. He thought he might faint. It was the kind of news that would knock any man down. "My daughter? My son-in-law? Little Tia too? A chip truck?" In their little car, he knew they never stood a chance. *It can't be*, he thought as he looked around at their moving boxes by the front door. His daughter and husband and sweet little granddaughter had gone to get some things for the new home they would be moving into. In one horrible moment, those plans had changed.

A shoe, a wallet, a baby's pacifier, all strewn across the highway. How could things have gone so terribly wrong? One minute this little family was on its way back to Grandma and Grandpa's; the next the father and daughter were gone, and the mother was fighting to survive at a local hospital. Hadn't God seen them?

* * *

A carpenter's tool, sandals, and the chair he had made for Mary's birthday. Strewn about the house, this is all that was left of Lazarus. How could things have gone so terribly wrong? One minute he was out working in the shed on a carpentry project; the next minute Lazarus was gone, encased in rubble. Hadn't God seen him?

* * *

Ashes, ashes, and more unformed substance. Strewn across the Manhattan streets, this is all that was left of the lives of some 2,000 people. How could things have gone so terribly wrong? One minute they were at their office desks; the next minute they were gone—all of them, encased in rubble. Hadn't God seen them?

* * *

A family wiped out by a chip truck.

Lazarus' sudden death.

Two thousand buried beneath the World Trade Center.

Each scenario leaves a gut-wrenching ache behind as a thieving bird swoops down and carts off what's precious to us. It's at those moments, when Goliath flies off with our treasure in tow, that's it's tempting to call it quits on this thing called faith.

But not the Habakkuk heart.

Just as the floodwaters are cresting, the Habakkuk heart snags its footing onto something solid in the mighty current. Something has a hold of them. Something is holding them back from being swept down river in a torrent of despair. It's an altar in the deep.

* * *

"Where's Don and Tia?" she asked groggily from her

hospital bed. It hurt to move. It hurt to blink. Though she had been told to conserve her strength, she needed to find out where her husband and baby were.

"Susan, they're in heaven," she heard someone say. She shut her eyes. Maybe it was just a bad dream. But the awful memory of tires squealing brought her back to reality. She opened her eyes. Her body was racked with pain, IV bottles hung over her head, and tubes ran through the bed railing to and from her arms. Arms. Her arms felt empty without Tia. She looked back to the family members standing by her bed.

"They're in heaven," she was assured again. A tear rolled down her cheek.

"I hoped so," she said. *At least they're not suffering,* she thought.

It was too much for darkness to handle. *Worship at a time like this?* squawked darkness as it flew away. With one foot in heaven with her husband and baby girl, and one foot on earth with her extended family, Susan scribbled grace in the midst of floodwaters. it was a message her family and friends needed as they attended her funeral. It was a note from the deep—from an altar in the deep.

* * *

Some 20 years later, Susan's faith helps those left behind make out the shoreline of heaven; her words skip like pebbles, turning deep-water grief into works of art.

Tupperware was made for grieving women. The day my

Uncle Vern passed away, mine took a real beating. My uncle was a tall, quiet man. I loved the way he carried himself. While some men *have* to say something, Uncle Vern was a man who had something to say—and still wouldn't. Just a humble guy, he took the time to watch me shoot baskets when I was a lanky, uncoordinated kid. Even when I was crummy at it, he made me believe I was good. He didn't live in the same town, but he made it a point to come to my games. Later on, he came to some of my own kids' games.

When he passed away, I headed to the kitchen.

The way women in my family—and I suspect most families—deal with sorrow is by cooking. Call it the nurturing instinct. Whatever it is, we women have a built-in drive to fix whatever it is that's troubling our families and friends, and if we can't fix their sorrows, the least we can do is eliminate a few hunger pains. So we go to the kitchen. We work out our grief by beating a few eggs, pounding out some dough, or chopping up a head of lettuce.

But it's the Tupperware that takes the brunt of a sorrowing woman. Misty-eyed, we dig like bulls through what was once a fairly well-organized Tupperware cupboard. Deep inside our Tupperware caves we can let loose our tears, and no one's the wiser. At our altars in the deep, we admit our anger. We get real with God. We get honest before the Lord, We dig, we send a few pieces flying against the sidewalls, and we pray. Finally. we emerge a little less burdened and with just the right size and shape container into which we slip our balm of Gilead for the family.

Had Martha, Lazarus's sister, had Tupperware, it would have taken a beating the day her brother died. Martha always fixed whatever it was that was ailing her family. The day her brother died, she no doubt headed to the kitchen. She probably pounded out some bread dough. *If only He had been here, Lazarus wouldn't have died,* she cried as she searched for the perfect bowl in which to place her dough.

She was sad. She was angry. She felt robbed. Death had swooped in like a terror from the skies and stolen away someone she treasured. And Jesus had been out of town when it happened.

"Perfect timing," she muttered through her tears. She wanted her brother back. She dug through the cupboard, remembering that it was the very cupboard Lazarus had built for her. She stroked the wood and thought about what a great brother he had been to her.

Tears rolled. She continued rummaging through the wooden bowls. It wasn't about finding the perfect bowl. It *never is* for a woman. It was about pounding out some grief. Martha, practical Martha, had gone looking for God in her own way.

Outside, family and friends gathered along the stone wall that ran along the front of their home. Mary, Martha's sister, ran by them, weeping. Supposing that she was headed to the tomb to weep there, the company followed her. But Mary had been watching the horizon. Spotting Jesus from afar, she bolted to meet Him. He had just gotten back into town.

She could barely see through her tears as she ran sobbing, but she recognized Him. Everything would be all right if she could just get to Him. Out of breath, she stumbled the last few yards and fell at His feet. "Lord, if you had been here, my brother would not have died," she whimpered.

He knelt and lifted her up by the shoulders. In His hands He could feel her tremble. Her grief pierced His heart. His brow furrowed with concern. He lifted her chin and intently scanned her face. Wiping the dirt and tears from her cheek, He sighed and held her more firmly by the shoulders. She was too undone to speak. From her trusting eyes fell tears of sorrow.

"Lazarus—gone!" Mary whimpered. His bottom lip trembled. Death had swooped in and taken His friend Lazarus, and now it was clawing at Mary. He hated how it was tearing her apart; it made Him weep.

God hates death. It made Him angry. It made Him sorrow. It made Him roll up His sleeves, march to Lazarus's tomb, and shout, "Lazarus, come out!" God demanded death give back what it had swooped in and stolen. Sometimes we forget that God hates death more than we do. It troubles Him deeply to see death steal away His treasured creations and break the hearts of those left behind.

Inside every heart, God has placed eternity. Something tells us we should live forever—that our friends and family members shouldn't die. Life is too precious to suddenly end, just end. God thinks so too. It wasn't part of His original plan. Eternal life was what He had in mind. God didn't include death in the blueprint for the Garden of Eden.

He did, however, take a risk when He designed human beings with free will rather than robots He could manipulate. When God designed that type of creatures, there was a risk that they might choose to exalt themselves and their own opinions over their Maker's. And they did.

* * *

"There must have been plenty of other trees," observed one of my little Sunday School kids one Sunday morning. She's right. There were plenty of other trees in the Garden of Eden. There was an abundance of food with heavenly flavors. God had given Adam and Eve everything they could have wanted and more. Still, they wanted the one thing they couldn't have, the forbidden tree. They felt they knew better than God. They doubted God's goodness and took the fruit. They exalted themselves against their Creator and His original design.

At that moment, selfish sin unlocked Goliath's door, and he's been out roaming and orchestrating funerals on this earth ever since. But God in His compassion has made a way of escape for the humanity who brought death to this world. In the river bed of our deep sin, God built an altar. On it, He laid His son.

Jesus Christ's death and resurrection rolled back the deep torrents of sweeping sin and reversed the cursing tides demanding our lives. We can now cross safely on dry ground from death to life. Humanity has been given a second chance at eternal life, a second chance at an eternal Garden of Eden, a life God had in mind in the original blueprint.

We get to choose whether we anchor our lives to the altar in the deep or whether the dark waters sweep over us and we're drug back with Goliath to his dark dungeon of pain and sorrow and suffering for all eternity. The thought of us there causes Christ to weep. The thought of us there caused Him to roll up His sleeves and go make a way of escape.

* * *

It was a story told at one of my son's basketball camps. A deadly earthquake hit a small village. A little boy in that village was trapped under twisted rubble with some other people. They were alive but trapped. The people began to despair—but not the little boy.

"Don't worry—my father will come," he assured them. Hours passed. Again the little boy said, "My father is coming for us." Tenderly, the others explained to him that his father did love him but that he may not know how to get to them. But the little boy insisted, "My father is coming. He *is*!"

Not wanting to crush his little-boy hopes, they left him to his comforting illusion. When it looked as though all hope was lost, they heard the sound of someone peeling back the layers of rubble. Soon a shaft of daylight broke forth and poured down on them. It was the little boy's father. He reached down and grabbed his son and drew him into a hug, so thankful that he was alive. As the others made their way out, they told the father of his son's insistent hope. He looked his boy in his eyes and smiled with joy that he had found him. "I told them you were coming," said the little boy.

Just like that earthly father, we have a Heavenly Father who looked down and saw how sin buried us in a rubble tomb. He sent His best. He sent His Son. And that Son ran a great distance to reach us. He sprinted. Nothing was going to stop Him from setting us free from hell's grip.

* * *

It was a dark dungeon; "hell on earth" was how some described "Ground Zero." To this day, the 2001 terrorist attacks on the Twin Towers in New York City assault the human senses. Life was there one minute and gone the next. Our human hearts still have difficulty handling the idea of life disintegrating with all its functioning building blocks and complicated DNA. The pulse in our veins, the rise and fall of our chests as we breathe, hold us captive and unable to entertain the thought of such destruction of human life. Our heads won't compute it. Our eyes can't believe it. Our hearts won't take it in. Such precious life perishing beyond detection is just too much for the soul to consider. That day we needed someone bigger than us. We needed a miracle. We needed a miracle-worker.

That same year my husband and I were expecting our third child. With two boys, I secretly wondered if this would be our girl! But another boy would be great too. We tucked the first ultrasound picture into our Bible—the first "baby picture." The sound of the heartbeat made it all the more real that we would be parents again soon. Our due date was right at Christmas time.

A perfect gift, we said, smiling. We thought of a few names: Kelli, or maybe Page. For the most part, we kept our excitement to ourselves. Then one day the dream died. At two months we miscarried. Life was there one minute and gone the next. We needed someone bigger than us. We needed a miracle. We needed a miracle-worker.

* * *

On the third day a miracle happened.

"They've run out of wine," Jesus' mother whispered into her son's ear. Looking around the room, Jesus spotted six stone water pots on a shelf in the corner.

"Fill the water pots with water," He told His disciples. So they filled them to the brims. "Draw some out now, and take it to the headwaiter."

When the headwaiter tasted the water that had become wine and wondered where it came from, the headwaiter called the bridegroom and said to him, "Every man usually serves the good wine first, and when the people have drunk freely, then he serves the poorer wine; but you have kept the best wine for last!"

Of all the miracles that Jesus could have started His ministry with, one would have thought that His first miracle would have been something other than changing water into wine. Turning water into wine seems a little lackluster, doesn't it? It did help the wedding party at Cana save face,

I suppose, but what larger good did it serve? Why didn't Jesus start with a miracle like walking on water? That's a show-stopper! Better yet, why not do something really useful like healing the blind or raising the dead? Why start His ministry by turning water into wine at a wedding?

At first glance it does seem a bit dull. But when you think about it some more, you can see that it's possibly the most powerful and hope-filled miracle of all. Changing water into wine lets us know we have a God who is in charge of things on a molecular level. The best minds and bioengineers of today can't convert H_2O molecules into wine molecules. It just can't be done.

But Jesus did it.

He alone is in charge of things on a micro-level, on a level the human eye cannot see, on a level where the DNA and building blocks of life are, on a level where life exits, on a level where your life beats and breathes.

When tragedy leaves nothing of a precious loved one to identify or bury—whether from a personal miscarriage or a global attack—we can remember that our loved one's frame is not hidden from God. It's not hidden from the God who changed water into wine and can reconstruct things on a molecular level.

"Your eyes have seen my unformed substance," declares Ps. 139:16. God's eyes have seen. He has taken careful notice. And what greater validation upon human life is there than the gaze of the Almighty, who long ago set His gaze upon the world and hated death and its terror so much that He placed His Son on a Cross—on an altar in the deep? For those who have placed their faith in him, there's not a rubble tomb that can hold them, not a terror from the sky that can steal their treasures.

In Joshua's day, two altars at two different locations were built: one in the middle of the deep river and the other in a more convenient location. The Bible tells us in the Book of Joshua that the altar he built in the middle of the Jordan River is still there to this very day. Have you ever wondered what those rough and rugged stones stacked long ago in the middle of that riverbed might look like after so many years of rough currents? Like the rocks that come out of my son's rock tumbler, all smooth and polished with their amazing banding and eye-catching flecks of sparkle, one can only imagine the beauty of that altar in the deep and those who are called to worship there.

CODE RED

FACING TRAGEDY ON THE MISSION FIELD

Teach me to trod this soil, Father,
With both feet making tracks in heaven.

—Jody

I GREW UP SPENDING MY SUMMERS on a boat dock. My parents owned a lake cabin right on the waters of Coeur D' Alene Lake in Idaho. All five of us kids, plus however many friends we could stuff into our Suburban, headed to the lake most every weekend. I lived for the smell of the pine trees and the giant inner tubes we rolled down the winding steps leading from our cabin to the swimming area below. We played "king of the rock," bouncing each other off the tubes into the water. My brother always won.

Around noon, the smell of hot dogs on the grill mingled in an oddly wonderful way with the boat fumes from the docks. Suddenly starved, we darted up the steps to our cabin, grabbed a dog, and dug into mom's creamy potato salad. With lunch wolfed down, we would snag a soda from the fridge, the portable radio from one of the bedrooms, and hit the lake for the afternoon. At night we draped our lake-drenched towels over the railing and fell into our bunks and drifted off to sleep to the lapping of the water against the docks below. The next day we did it all over again.

Mornings at the cabin were entertaining. They began with sliding a plastic bowl full of Cocoa Puffs out onto the deck. Out of sight behind the screen door, we would wait for the punctual arrival of a friendly chipmunk that never failed to climb a nearby tree trunk and come stuff his cheeks to bulging with the cereal.

Everything was brighter at the lake. The water was clear, the air crisp, and the pine trees were a fresh green.

The night sky sparkled—especially on the 4th of July. That was when every neighbor, having swung through the reservation on the way to the lake, purchased for a nominal price an abundance of fireworks. Just before dark, we would slip into our flip flops, grab a flashlight, and head down to the docks. With the smell of cocoa butter still on our skin, we ushered in the night's activities by lighting sparklers and boldly writing our names on the darkness.

Soon every cabin surrounding the lake, one by one, in overlapping rhythm, sent their fireworks streaking across the sky. "Wow—look at that one!" murmured onlookers as red and blue sprays of whistling lights illuminated the sky and the waters below. The whole lake sparkled like diamonds. Within hours the amazing display was done—gone. The lake lit by only the moon, we sat on the dock, not wanting the evening to be over.

Instinctively, we longed for the luminosity that filled the night sky. We longed for the way those lights lifted our heads, the way they lit up our faces and the faces of our friends, the way they caused us to snuggle under blankets with family, the way they filled our hearts with squealing delight, wonder, and awe. In those lights there was an eternal quality. We knew they should last forever. It's what made us sigh when it was all done. It's what kept us coming back to the docks each July.

* * *

In the early 1900s, Henrietta Leavitt blew the dust off the ledge of her observatory window, set her pencil down, and rubbed the back of her neck. Taking a brief break from her telescope, she leaned against one of the observatory's corner posts and peered into the bustling night life. It was a beautiful, starry, night. Streetlights lit the edges of Harvard University's campus. Below, people milled about in the warm summer breeze.

Edward Pickering had recruited Henrietta himself. Reserved for only the most serious students, Harvard was filled mainly with men. Henrietta was a rare exception. On weekends, however, there were more women on campus than usual. Men left their dorm rooms and spent a fun evening with one of the many flapper girls who had come to stroll the campus.

I have a date with the stars, she said to herself as she picked up her pencil and stepped back onto the platform of the observatory. *I want to catalogue one more star before daylight.* With her pencil in her mouth, she set to work, peering into the heavens. She wanted to determine how long it would take for the star in her scope to go from very dim to very bright.

This was her seventh night observing this particular star. One of the other stars she had watched had taken 70 days to go from dim to bright, another star only four. Across the top of her journal were written the words "Periods of Luminosity." Each star had its own unique period—she was sure of it. Maybe it was her upbringing in the church her father pastored, or maybe it was just her gut faith in an orderly Creator, but something told her that every star was unique. Even if no one else at Harvard believed her hunch, she did. If it took every night of her life, she was going to find each star's unique period of luminosity and turn her faith-driven hunch into a scientific fact.

Henrietta couldn't hear the flirting horns of Model T cars cruising in the distance, making their way to the local theater. She was deaf. The sounds of the Roaring Twenties were lost to Henrietta. She found the theater of the night sky, however, plenty engaging. She could hear the drumbeat beauty of the heavens above. Each star was too mechanical, too rhythmic in nature, too uniquely orderly for there not to be a Designer behind it.

Unfathomable order, she mused as she took the chewed pencil from her mouth. She couldn't calculate the distance of the next star until she calculated the distance of the star in front of it. *Each star's period of luminosity seems to determine the distance to the next star and ultimately the distance on out to the universe.* She took the pencil from her mouth and scribbled a few notes to herself.

Looking into the sky, she smiled with delight. Could it be that she had just devised a yardstick by which to measure the heavens? The mice living in the planks of the observatory's walls peeked out and twitched their whiskers, as if sensing something in the air. *That ought to suit Mr. Pickering,* Henrietta sassily thought as she logged another star in her Periods of Luminosity notebook.

While others were out and about in Ford's latest powered invention, the edges of Henrietta's hoop skirt swept the wooden planks of Harvard's observatory well into the night. Oblivious to what others found entertaining, she continued her rendezvous with the stars, her nocturnal friends in the corner, and the Creator behind it all.

* * *

Heating up and cooling down is part of a star's life. So it is with our lives. When a star is in its shrink and heat stage of intense pressure, it is at its most luminous stage. Ironically, it is at that most difficult stage that a star is at its grandest. Just as it seems it might blow apart under the pressure, something causes it to tip back and expand to cooling.

Maybe you know what it means to be under intense pressure. One minute life is grand and your faith is unshakable, and the next minute it's hard to say what life's about other than a lot of pressure. Look up! The heavens proclaim His glory, but not without a lot of intense pressure—nuclear pressure at that. You may not realize it, but like the stars above, your faith and life shine brightest when under the most pressure. It's there in the luminous shrink and heat stage, the stage of intense pressure, that things are most luminous.

What period of luminosity are you in? Has it been a one- or two-day heat and shrink period? Or has God trusted you with an intense 70-day cycle? Don't give up. That shrink and heat stage is for a brief moment in time; it shall pass. It's designed for a purpose you may not be able to measure from your perspective in the galaxy.

Fortunately, the stars above have a tipping point, where just as it seems they might explode from pressure, a mechanism unknown to scientists tip them back to a cooling cycle. This tipping point in the cosmos is called "hydrostatic equilibrium." Scientists don't understand why it happens—they just know that all stars experience hydrostatic equilibrium. Their existence, like ours, is a ping pong between mountaintop experiences and valley experiences. At the end of their existence, stars become dwarf stars or giant stars. Dwarf stars, particularly black dwarf stars, don't shine. They don't experience any pressure to shine. They become burnt-out balls of ash that inspire nothing around them. Giant stars, on the other hand, experience intense nuclear pressure, some enough to explode into a blaze of light called a supernova, the most awe-inspiring lights in the universe.

When it comes to suffering, we have only two choices. We can choose to trust God with the process of suffering, the intense heat and shrink stages of our lives, or we can turn our backs on God and become bitter, burnt-out balls of ash: black dwarfs.

Your suffering is the result of a fallen world where the original sin of the garden unlocked the giants' door and where Goliaths now roam and play havoc in our lives.

God hates the roaming giants as much as you do. The intense pull they create on your life and your faith can be taxing. You may feel out of whack and that life is out of equilibrium, but you have only to look up into the stars to understand that only God can take your faith-filled suffering and weave it with the faith-filled sufferings of others and create a constellation of glory you can't possibly measure from your vantage point. Your supernova existence is part of a canopy of lights that can't be measured from your location in space.

* * *

She pulled back from her scope. It was almost daybreak. One lone star lingered in the morning sky. *You never sleep, Venus, you bright and morning star,* thought Henrietta as she gave a yawn. The fingers of dawn stretched across Harvard's campus below, and slowly switching off each campus light. Though she couldn't hear the melody of the birds singing their morning song, she knew it was time to call it a night. She stretched and yawned again, as did her friends in the walls. Lifting her hoop skirt, she made her way off the observatory's platform, grabbed her cloak hanging on a tall coat rack in the corner of the room, and wound her way down the lonely staircase. There were always the same Goliaths waiting for her at the bottom of the steps. Her work usually kept her mind off them. But there they were again to greet her day.

Deafness.

Cancer.

There they stood in the morning light with their smug looks. One would spend the day stripping her from the beauty of ever hearing a bird's song or a friend's comforting words; the other would attack her dignity one thinning hair at a time. Henrietta squinted into the morning light and kept her gaze heavenward. She could see a sliver of the Bright and Morning Star and thought of her Savior. *I'm glad you never sleep—I need your strength,* she prayed as she plucked another loose hair from the sleeve of her jacket and walked back to her dorm room.

Henrietta passed away in 1921 from the Goliath of cancer. Her friends and family described her as quiet and reserved in every way except in her praise for the Creator behind the stars she studied. Goliath never stole her worship. Her Habakkuk heart praised God despite her deafness and cancer. She knew everything happened for a reason and that God would work all things together for good, just as He did with the stars above. The scientist in her, as well as her own faith, told her that people's lives, like stars, differed from one another in their glory.

"There is one glory of the sun, and another glory of the moon, and another glory of the stars, for star differs from star in glory" (1 Cor. 15:41). Some people who are full of faith are healed, and some people who are full of faith are *not* healed. All are created to give God glory. In 1925, after her passing, Henrietta was awarded the Nobel Prize. Because of her work, scientists have a yardstick by which they can attempt to measure the universe.

Solon Baily eulogized Henrietta in these words: "Miss Leavitt had a happy faculty of appreciation for all that was worthy and lovable in others and was possessed of a nature so full of sunshine that, to her, all of life became beautiful and full of meaning."

* * *

Colors of nausea swept over her. The purposes for her going to Croatia seemed to dim with each cringing swallow of her swollen throat. She felt like throwing up. *Maybe if I lie in the seat back, I'll feel better,* she thought. It was going to be a long road trip to Portland from her home in Wendell, Idaho. She was glad her mom was with her.

"How about we listen to some music as we drive?" her mom said, comforting. At 26, Katie was surprised she had a fondness for old hymns; they never failed to bring peace to her mind and heart. She reclined her seat. Music did make her feel better. They were meeting up with the rest of the Campus Crusade for Christ team in Portland. Katie and the team had been planning the trip for months. Croatia, a small country near Bosnia, was their destination. It was a country full of old cities, cobblestone streets, and fortified walls. The Croatian flag resembled a chessboard with alternating squares of red and white.

Feeling as she was, she wondered if going was a wrong move. *Checkmate,* taunted her nausea. She cracked the window for some fresh air, determined to outsmart her queasy stomach. Doubt tried to claim her piece by piece as it whispered, *How are you going to be of help to anyone in this shape?*

"Mom, could you turn the music up a bit?" she asked

in an effort to hush her nagging thoughts. *Comb, toothbrush, passport, extra socks,* she said to herself, mentally repacking her suitcase. Her propensity for detail and organization helped her pass the time.

Abba, what is this sickness? she prayed as she looked out her window. From her reclined seat, her line of vision peered above the rim of the car door straight up into the overcast sky. The morning star was still out. She stared at it as the rocking motion of the car swayed her into prayer. *I'm with you, Katie, day and night,* spoke the Lord to her heart.

My throat is so swollen, Lord, that I feel I'm going to gag. Please help me to feel better. There was little to do but listen to music, pray, and watch the clouds through the window. She closed her eyes.

Sunlight broke free from the clouds and streamed through the window, bathing her in its warmth. She opened her eyes and smiled. She felt peace cover her worries, cover her body, cover her journey. *Thank you, Jesus, my Bright and Morning Star,* she prayed as she closed her eyes again and fell asleep with the fingers of sunlight dancing across her cheeks.

After joining her team in Portland, they began settling into their motel rooms. It was nice to finally be with the friends who shared the same vision. She didn't feel any better; in fact, she felt even worse, but at least she was with her team. With her things unpacked enough for the evening, she thought she would turn in a little early and get a good night's sleep before the team flew to Europe the next morning.

The next day she forced herself to fight the fatigue and grab an early shower before meeting the others for breakfast. The hot steam fogged the mirror. *This feels so good on my throat.* She stood under the shower head and allowed the water to pour over her head. She was tempted to stay there in the steam for the rest of the day. It would certainly be good for the tonsillitis the doctors thought she was fighting.

With the click of the faucet, she reached out through the curtain and grabbed a couple of towels, one to dry with and wrap around her, and the other to wrap around her hair. She pulled the curtain back and stepped out onto the bathroom rug. Her things lined the bathroom counter like an orderly constellation: her toothbrush and paste in a baggie on the right-hand side, her medicine for her throat on the other side near her drinking cup, and her hairbrush and toiletries neatly arranged across the top. Everything had a home and everything was in its home.

That's how she liked it—orderly. Padding out of the bathroom with her hair pulled up in a towel and wearing a pair of comfy, oversized, black sweatpants and a t-shirt, she had just enough time to slip in a devotional before breakfast. Retrieving her bag from the corner, she sat down on the bed. Queasy, she took a deep breath and sat still. Everything dimmed. *What good am I here?* she said, exhaling.

After a few minutes, she pulled her Bible from her

bag and began reading. Then she pulled out two pens. One was blue, the other red. Instinctively, she picked up the blue one, folded over the next page in her journal, and began writing:

Sunday, November 27, 2005

Portland, OR

Abba, what is this sickness? Where does it come from? It gets worse each day, no matter what the doctors do. It should be so much better today, yet it is worse than it has ever been. My throat is so swollen that my tonsils and epiglottis are touching, and I want to gag at every moment. The only times I have felt better are driving in the car with Mom, sleeping in the sun and listening to hymns, and when Amy Peterson prayed for me.

Lord, I'm scared. Help me not to panic. For whatever reason, Satan is opposing my going to Croatia. I don't know why. I am so out of it. I find myself unable to focus more than a moment at a time. I don't see what purpose this sickness is serving. Is my purpose in coming here really to be miserable and a drain on the team rather than an encouragement and blessing? I don't understand.

But I do know that greater is He that is in me than he that is in the world. I know that you are in control. Help me to live that belief, Lord. For your name and glory.

Setting her blue pen aside, she picked up the red pen.

Something always happened when she picked up the red pen. She couldn't explain it. It was as if they were pens from two different time zones, from two different worlds, a heavenly one, an earthly one. Impressions from another place, a heavenly place, moved in red ink.

Oh, my beloved, I am here with you in the midst of this. Do not fear. All is well and will be well. You will be well again. You will be healed. Rejoice in the reality that it is my will to heal your body.

Rejoice in the reality that it is my will for you to go to Croatia. Fully and completely, you are going according to my will. Trust in that. Trust in me, beloved, when the fear and panic set in. Trust in me and meditate on my Word. Trust in me and do not be afraid. I love you, Katie. It is my will for you to get on that plane. What I have for you in Croatia is not all about productivity or getting things done.

—Jesus

* * *

Katie flew out with her team after breakfast. She made it to Croatia during the summer of 2005. Within days of her arrival, however, just shy of her 27th birthday, this young college girl with a heart for God came home in a casket. The Goliath of leukemia seemed victorious as it turned an overseas mission trip into a nightmare.

Wasn't God interested in reaching the lost and protecting His servants who were just trying to obey the Great

Commission? *How unfair for it to play out this way!* whispered the darkness. But a louder voice could be heard coming from the pages of Katie's journal. It was the hopeful voice of the Habakkuk heart. The red ink strung across those pages had become a code. It told anyone and everyone who read it exactly where God was. It was full of Katie's last candid thoughts. It was her faith, written in red. It was fellowship on paper.

Though her pen could have been filled with bitterness from the dim realities of her weakening body, Katie's Habakkuk heart had spoken not about a distant God who didn't care but about a God who was in control, about a God who had never left her side, about a God who was working a plan, a productive and orderly plan, just as Katie had hoped.

So deeply anchored within the veil of heaven was Katie's Habakkuk heart that even in her final days there was no lack of confidence that God was in control. As friends slid under each arm and helped her down a flight of stairs, Katie salted their concerned looks with "Look—God has answered our prayer for team unity!" Laughing through tears, they made their way down the winding steps and placed her in a taxi cab. "We love you, Katie," said her friends as they tenderly buckled her in. It was the last time they saw her alive.

Katie's journal was an undeniable light, an incredibly transparent interaction between heaven and earth where the fireworks of her faith blazed across the night sky of doubt. It's hard to believe Katie is gone. Instinctively, family and friends still go back and linger over the pages of her journal. Not wanting her light to be over, they sit and remember. They long for the way her life lit up their faces, the way she had a basket to organize everything in her apartment, the way she loved a pair of oversized sweatpants. "I know they're ugly, but they're so comfy," she would tell them as she fixed her Bible study group a plate of nachos or pulled some cookies from her oven. There was something eternal about her. They knew it.

Maybe your life is going backward instead of forward. Maybe you wonder how you could possibly be a good influence on anyone around you. Maybe your days seem less than productive. As Katie went to her watchtower of prayer, so can you. Be real. He already knows your thoughts. Be transparent. Tell your Creator your frustrations. Don't hold back. Get real with your Maker. Katie did. She ran like the ancient prophet, Habakkuk. She ran to her watchtower of prayer, her Bible and her journal, and showed her Maker the inner workings of her heart. *What good am I to anyone here?* she cried out to God. And He reminded her that His reasons for bringing her there weren't all about what she could do for Him—rather, they were about what He could do through her when she had no strength left.

The Campus Crusade for Christ organization will forever be touched by Katie Walsh. Fellow members describe her death as dramatic. It happened on foreign soil. It happened without warning. What's more, they mourn the fact that she died alone in a hospital room. The bureaucratic tape of foreign soil was such that friends, however close, were not family and were therefore not permitted into the ICU wing. It haunts them that it played out that way. She was too much a people person to have passed away behind fortified walls without friends by her side. Katie is remembered for how she spent her last days, traveling thousands of miles and crossing oceans and distant lands for no other reason than to tell others about the distance a King ran to call her His own.

She left behind a treasure, a code of sorts: a red cord that loops across the pages of her journal. It's a cord that friends and family have needed to climb out of what seems a senseless pit. It's a cord by which they hoist themselves up into the confidence that God is good. God did have a plan for Katie, and He calls each one of us for His glory, for purposes we will one day see. For now, we cling to the red cord of faith Katie lowered over the ledge of her Croatian hospital room. Through the window of her journal we see a good God.

* * *

She lowered the thick red cord out her window. "Good morning, little bird." He cocked his head her way and continued pecking about the thick window ledge jutting out in front of her window. Her room was in the top right-hand corner of Jericho's fortified walls. She liked the view. She could see out over the green hills from up here.

It was just a floor away from the rooftop. Sometimes at night she wrapped a shawl around her shoulders and went up to the roof. From there she could see the city's torch lights illuminating the cobblestone street below. She could spend an entire evening just people-watching.

But that's not what drew Rahab to the roof. She couldn't explain it, but beneath the manifold witness of the stars she felt the nearness of Jehovah, the Israelite God. *There—they ought to see that,* she thought as she finished securing the crimson cord in place. When the Israelites stormed the faithless city, they would see it and spare her life.

It was more than a cord. It was a code. In essence, it was her faith written in red. With her faith on the line, she and her whole household would be saved. Little did she know that her confession of faith would cover her sins and graft her into the lineage of Christ, where she would become the great-grandmother, many times removed, of the royal Jesus Christ.

There is something that is a brighter crimson red than our sins—the blood of Christ. His cord of love and sacrifice has been lowered from the window ledge of heaven. When we confess the sins of our wayward hearts that have cheated on God, when we confess how we've put other loves before that of our Creator, His working rope falls into our grasp and hoists us up from the pit of separation, up onto the window ledge of heaven—where God is, where the Bright and Morning Star, Jesus Christ himself, is, where everything has a home and everything is in its home.

9
PATHFINDERS
FACING HEALTH ISSUES

*To the most faithful does God sometimes
entrust the steepest of valleys.*

—Jody

SHE WAS ALL OF 10 and had the cutest freckles across the bridge of her nose. She sat before me on the reading rug with her hand raised high above her grin. "Mrs. Conrad, I have a prayer request!" I opened our spiral notebook and dated a new page. My fourth-graders had almost filled the 80-cent wide-ruled notebook with their Sunday morning prayer requests.

"Yes, Maia—please share with us," I said, encouraging her. She and her family had just moved to the country, and knowing her love for animals, I steadied my pen, expecting her to request prayer for one of the many animals she had come to care for on their farm.

"Well," she began, "my baby brother prayed the silliest prayer last night that made my dad and mom and all of us laugh," she said, giggling. The rest of the ten-year-olds seated on the rug now turned and gave Maia their full attention, wondering what silly prayer her four-year-old brother had prayed. Being 10, they knew better than to pray silly prayers.

"He prayed," Maia said and then mimicked her little brother's baby voice, "'Tank you, God, for kitties we can dwag frew da dirt!'" The class erupted in laughter.

With my pen stalled on the notebook paper, I chuckled. In my mind's eye I could see her little brother walking around their farm with his baseball cap on and a cat innocently slung over his shoulder like Linus from the comic strip *Peanuts*, who walked around with a blue blanket draped over his shoulder. *Thank you, God, for kitties we can drag through the dirt* didn't quite look right on paper, but there it was. We needed to get to our Sunday School lesson. So we bowed our heads and quickly prayed and thanked God for the wonders of farm life.

As the kids rushed from the reading rug to their chairs around the classroom table, I closed the spiral notebook. We now knew exactly why cats need nine lives. I was sure I could hear God chuckle.

None of us has nine lives. But we probably all know what it's like to be dragged around against our will. Bumping along upside-down, face-first through the dirt can cause a person to lose perspective. It's hard to see where you're headed in that position. It's hard to keep any sort of eternal perspective. It's even more difficult to keep some semblance of hope. In that position, despair and hopelessness have the upper hand.

* * *

Her situation teetered on the edge of hopelessness. One minute she was standing at the kitchen sink doing a few dishes, looking through her kitchen window enjoying the flowers in her garden, and the next she was on the kitchen floor.

She couldn't breathe.

She couldn't move.

It was as if something had hold of her throat and her head—her very life. Her husband, walking through the kitchen side-door, spotted her on the kitchen floor and rushed to her side. Something was desperately wrong. He cradled her in his arms and dialed 911.

"Be sure to get the salad to church," she whispered.

Within minutes they found themselves in an ambulance slowly making its way through the delays of road construction.

"You're going to be OK," he assured her as he held her hand.

Judy had just completed 30-some years as a kindergarten teacher. In celebration, they had planned a trip to Branson, Missouri, by train. It seemed like the perfect way to begin their retirement years. Now they found themselves in the middle of an emergency. This wasn't the trip they had planned.

"You're going to make it," encouraged her husband. The golden years didn't look so golden. Time was ticking, the sun was setting. There was nothing he could do. There was nothing anybody could do. The torn-up road before them was eating up critical minutes. Everyone knew it. Whatever had hold of Judy seemed to be winning. She needed medical attention and now.

Just ahead seemed to be a glimmer of hope. Like a scene from a movie, neighbors circled their cars and pickup trucks in an open field and used their headlights to guide the overhead medical chopper down safely. It seemed like the perfect solution, that is until the unfamiliar sights and sounds of the chopper blades spooked a group of horses grazing in the pasture below. Landing in a rural setting was proving to be a bit too risky. The chopper would need to be waved off. They continued on at a grueling pace.

"Almost there, honey," he comforted.

Pushing through the bumpy construction, they finally arrived at the hospital, where Judy was rushed to open heart surgery. It was touch and go the first 48 hours. But she survived.

After many grueling months in the hospital and at rehabilitation centers, this 30-year veteran teacher is home now. Exercising on a stationary bike, she's determined to gain as much range of motion back in her hands and feet as possible. *I know you're with me, Lord,* she prays as she pedals her bike each day. Inactivity has never been her thing. When she wasn't teaching kindergarten, she was running lunches to the harvest field, working in her yard, canning, baking, or picking up grandkids. Her life was about others. It had always been about others. *Nothing is going to change that,* she thought as she pedaled and looked out the window.

The glare from a car bumper turning down the drive caught her eye. She stopped. Someone was coming for a visit. *It will be a nice break,* she thought as she wiped her brow and made her way from her stationary bike to her wheelchair.

For Judy, some things haven't changed at all. With grace and strength she faces her new challenge. But more than that, her life remains centered around others.

It was those others that she thought about that dreadful day as she lay on her kitchen floor barely able to breathe. "Be sure to get the salad to church." What kind of heart uses what could be her dying breath to voice the needs of others? What kind of faith bumps along upside down, face first through the dirt, and still thinks about others? The well-being of others came before her own well-being. Judy's faith tracked along deep ocean pathways not of this world.

* * *

It was considered precious cargo even by today's standards. In 1848 Captain Jackson unloaded it from his clipper ship onto the docks of Baltimore in record time.

"Bring 'em over 'ere, mates!" he shouted from the dock. He rubbed his stubbly chin and watched as his men unloaded the cargo of coffee down a narrow plank from the clipper ship to the dock. *A fine crew—a fine crew indeed.*

"There's one on me mates as soon as you're done!" he hollered before turning and making his way toward the many merchant houses and bars along Baltimore's waterfront.

"Hip, hip, hooray for Captain Jackson!" cheered a bunch of sailing blokes gathering for their morning coffee. The crowd had heard about Captain Jackson's amazing feat.

"Thirty-seven days—ain't dat right, Captain?" trailed the voice of one of his crewmembers as the men made their way into the storefront shop. Normally it would have taken another month to see a clipper ship deliver its cargo of coffee through the dangerous coastal waters around the tip of South Africa.

"Tell us, Captain—how'd ye steer her around the horn?" The maritimers perched with mugs in hand wanted to know. They knew those waters. The men sat riveted, waiting for Captain Jackson to share his sailing tale. They were anxious to hear how the Captain had sailed his vessel with such speed; many of them knew men who met their fate in those treacherous waters off the cape. "Tell us, Captain," the men said, jeering as they sat on the edges of their seats sipping at the coffee cups in their hands.

"First let Captain Jackson grab a little something to wet his whistle!" barked a sailor in the corner.

"My men come first," Captain Jackson said, gesturing toward his crew before pulling two pamphlets from a pocket inside his sailing jacket. The men pushed in for a closer look. Two pamphlets had guided Captain Jackson: *Wind and Current Charts* and *Sailing Directions*. They had been in publication only a year.

"Here's my secret, mates," Captain Jackson said as he plopped both pamphlets down for viewing. The mariners pushed in for a better view of the publications. "Mathew Fontaine Maury, men—that's the chap who wrote these," informed Captain Jackson. The men pored over the two pamphlets. They were full of inside information about trade winds, currents, and favorable sailing routes.

Mathew Fontaine Maury was a seasoned sailor who had documented hundreds of hours of naval observations in log books and who had recently published the findings in the two pamphlets. Among the observations, he noted the "favorable currents" along the Cape de Saõ Roque. His entire study of oceanography was driven by the truth he found in Ps. 8: that there were paths in the seas: "The birds of the heavens and the fish of the sea, Whatever passes through the paths of the seas" (Ps. 8:8).

He took seriously God's Word and often quoted it in the margins of his navigational records. He was sure God had placed pathways in the seas. So he went about spending his life as a detective of sorts. He found and mapped those pathways. Little did he know he would become Matthew Fontaine Maury, "Pathfinder of the Seas." Nor could he have imagined that commercial captains, seamen, and navy officers down through the ages would use his pamphlets to guide their ships through rough waters. They, too, would be able to tack through stormy waters with confidence that deep, unseen pathways were steering them from below.

"Where do we get a copy?" the men asked in unison.

"Well, Matthew Maury is wining and dining with dignitaries, all of whom want him to work for the naval department," Captain Jackson said. "They're calling Mr. Maury the father of oceanography. He's a bit busy right now, but we'll see if we can't get you blokes a copy of his two pamphlets."

The sailors didn't look up from the two pamphlets. They were too engrossed with the information before them.

Typically they headed their ships into open waters where it was calm. The calm waters added days to their journey around the cape but were much safer than the choppy waters near the coast, which they assumed were unnavigable. The pamphlet before them told a different story. While the coastline waters were unpredictable with their swirling whitecaps, the prevailing winds in that area near the south of Cape Horn revolved clockwise around a low-pressure center before reversing in a counterclockwise direction, allowing a sailing ship to tack back and forth through easterly winds around the Horn. A secret most sailors didn't know.

"Paths in the seas?" spouted one the sailors. "Crumb it all. We've been sailing days longer than we need be." They knew Maury's pamphlets would revolutionize their sailing. In them it explained, "The calm belts of the sea, like mountains on land, stand mightily in the way of the voyager. However, like mountains on the land, they have their passes and their gaps." That's why Captain Jackson had made such good time. Maury had instructed Captain Jackson to "stand boldly on, and if need be, tack, and work by under the land."

It was hard work, harder work than sailing his crew out into the open waters. But the determination paid off with a record-breaking sail of 37 days. Sailing the ship along the coastline required a diligent focus from every hand on board. With the swinging of the boom, everyone had to be in sync, or someone could get hurt.

In sailing terms, a "tack" or "coming about" requires a

considerable amount of speed by a sailing vessel and is a maneuver by which a ship turns its bow through sharp winds and rough waters in order to pitch the wind back and forth from one side of its sail to the other. To prepare a crew for the swinging of the boom, the skipper shouts, "Coming about!" The most important aspect of the maneuver is its attack speed. If the ship doesn't have enough speed to complete a tack, the wind may force the ship and its crew several lengths back into a previous course or stall the vessel altogether, which sailors refer to as being "in irons."

* * *

Maybe you're facing a situation in life in which you've simply lost steam and feel the winds pushing you back off course. You're putting up a good fight but losing ground by the minute. Or maybe things are worse than that. Maybe you've given up making any progress altogether. Life has stalled in rough waters and you're going nowhere fast.

In nautical terms, you're "in irons." There doesn't seem to be any hope. From your vantage point, rough waters and prevailing winds are as far as the eye can see. And as for the crew, you have no friends aboard your ship. You may be tempted to turn your collar up, pull your knees into your chest, and tuck your chin away from the biting winds. There's a part of you that wouldn't mind just jumping overboard. Don't give into that thought. It's from the enemy.

* * *

The Sea of Galilee delivered storms with Goliath-size wallops. One day the disciples found themselves in a horrendous one. Sheets of rain sleeted in sideways across the bow, making visibility difficult. Waves pitched the fishing boat back and forth, tossing the men around the water-filled deck like toy soldiers. With each crack of thunder, the storm grew worse. Against the blackening sky, the swells gulped down any hope of making it through.

"Master! Do you not care that we will perish?"

On a cushion in the stern of the pitching boat, Jesus slept. Their doubting shouts aroused Him, and He got up and rebuked the wind and said to the sea, "Hush—be still."

Immediately the winds died, and it became perfectly calm. The water was as still as glass. Still drenched by storm waters, the disciples stood, not knowing to what their fearful hearts belonged—the raging storm or the mighty hand of calm. Their hearts raced to catch up with their eyes. One minute a mighty storm seized their hearts; the next minute a mighty calm seized their hearts. Cold and wet, they dropped to their knees in reverence. *Who is this, that even the winds and the waves obey Him?* Their hearts flooded with wonder.

The only floodwaters that have touched my life were those the summer of 1987. Even then, I didn't experience the terror firsthand the way my mom and twin sister did. They were home alone at the time. Suddenly storm clouds blackened, lightning cracked, and the sky unleashed a floodwater of rain. The flash flood funneled a river of water through a draw behind our farmhouse. Within minutes, a wall of water, mud, and rock steamrolled into our home. Before it was over, an outdoor pool was leveled with mud and boulders, a car was picked up like a matchbox car by a river of water and deposited in the front yard. It was a powerful storm. The mud and water chased my mom and sister down a long hall to a back room in the house. As they hurried, they caught sight of a heavy freezer from the garage and the television set both floating in the nearby living room.

I don't know what it's like to have furious storm waters lick my heels, as my mom and sister and many others do. Many people in New Orleans cut holes into their attics and scrambled to the interiors of their roofs to escape the rising floodwaters caused by Hurricane Katrina. They say a flood is too frightening to put into words. I suppose it's the kind of terror the disciples felt that day on the Sea of Galilee. The storm waters raged all around them. There was no higher ground to escape to. They were terrified. Then something more powerful than the storm terrified them. With one rebuking "Hush," the Son of God stilled the raging storm waters. It terrified them. It caused them to marvel. It caused them to worship.

It wouldn't take any of us long to react as the disciples did and fall on our faces in worship at the sight of raging floodwaters becoming suddenly still. To have our trembling prayers answered in such a way, to have a life ring thrown in just as we're going down would cause the most critical skeptic to worship. It's safe to say that most of us would be filled instantly with grateful worship to see God hush the storm barreling down on top of us.

But what would our worship look like if the storm grew worse? Would we worship at all? Or would we just curse God?

Would we be filled with anger and bitterness toward God for not hushing our storm? Would we doubt His goodness should the floodwaters keep pouring in on top of us, flooding our boat? Embarrassingly enough, I'm afraid of what my heart might look like. To worship in the midst of catastrophic loss—that kind of Habakkuk worship dwelt in the heart of Job.

* * *

There was no "hush" that rebuked Job's storm. In fact, Job's storm *did* grow worse. Yet he still worshiped. He feared the mighty hand of God without benefiting from its staying power. What kind of person worships God after watching a raging storm take everything? Goliath winds tore a path of destruction from one end of his property to the other. His sons died. His daughters died. His servants and livestock were gone. Nothing was left.

Then Job rose, tore his robe, shaved his head, fell to the ground, and—cursed? No. Despaired? No. Worshiped? Yes. He worshiped! He prayed, "Naked I came from my mother's womb, And naked I shall return there. The LORD gave and the LORD has taken away. *Blessed* be the name of the LORD" (Job 1:21, emphasis added).

What kind of heart worships God when Goliath doesn't fall? What kind of heart blesses the Lord's name in the midst of tragedy? What kind of heart offers up praise as it bleeds? It's the kind of heart that arrests the heavens and fills angels with wonder.

Job's faith tacked through deep waters and hurricane winds. Then his friends came by and poured salt into his wounds. As he listened to them, he went from "tacking" through the storm of his life to being "in irons." They informed him that the storm wouldn't have happened if he hadn't done something to deserve it. Job was already down and out, and they came and delivered a good kick to the ribs. A law of attraction was at work, according to his friends, whereby prosperity followed those who followed God, and calamity followed those who were out of step with God. Then his friends got up and left Job to sit and think.

With the precision of a roadside surveyor, he analyzed the flawed elevations of his left arm for the next boil to scrape. He could feel the sun beating down on the back of his neck as he sat at the crest of the town dump. He continued scraping. Fortunately, there wasn't a lot of foot traffic in these parts. Every now and then, he glanced up and canvassed the dump. *Could be something down there to sleep on tonight.* He figured he had the rest of the day to look for an old mat. For now, he scraped and prayed and thought about what his friends said. Were they right? Had God abandoned him? Something in his Habakkuk heart said no.

He knew his God was in control. Still, he wondered

about the plans he had made. He and his wife were entering their golden years. Their kids were young adults. He had been looking forward to them taking over the livestock and raising families of their own. Now they were gone. So, too, were 7,000 sheep, 3,000 camels, 500 yoke of oxen, 500 female donkeys, and all the servants. The golden years didn't look so golden anymore. He continued to scrape and recalled the conversation he had had with his wife.

"Do you still hold fast your integrity? Curse God and die!" she said bitterly.

But he said to her, "You speak like a foolish woman. Shall we indeed accept good from God and not accept adversity?"

* * *

"Where have you come from?" asked God.

"From roaming about on the earth, and walking around on it," answered Satan.

And the Lord said to Satan, "Have you considered my servant Job? For there is none like him on the earth, a blameless and upright man fearing God and turning away from evil. And he still holds fast his integrity, although you incited me against him, to ruin him without cause."

"Skin for skin!" answered Satan. "Yes, all that a man has he will give for his life. However, put forth Your hand now, and touch his bone and his flesh; he will curse You to Your face!"

So the Lord said to Satan, "Behold, he is in your power, only spare his life" (*Job 2:2-6, adapted*).

* * *

From the top of the garbage dump a steady breeze picked up the scent of rotting material and wafted around Job's head. His skin began to erupt into larger boils. The air seemed more foul than before. With the condemning smell tagging his every breath, he continued to scrape each new bump. Though his bleeding skin told him that he had been ruined without cause, his faith tacked along deep ocean truths and told him that there was more to his life than what his eyes were seeing. His Habakkuk heart told him to trust in the unseen. He knew his God to be good. *God may have allowed all this to happen,* he reasoned, *but He wasn't the one who orchestrated this destruction. Someone, something, full of dark malice was behind this.* That much he knew. He set the potshard down. It was getting cold. He stood to his feet.

"Blessed be the name of the Lord!" he shouted across the lonely, stench-filled dump. A mocking silence sprawled before him. Night was falling. He needed to go look for that mat. But for a moment, the hues of the setting sun captured him. He didn't move. He just stared out over the nauseating fumes of the dump to the horizon line. In the sun's glorious exit of siren red, he could hear the voice of his Creator. God had not abandoned him after all.

Something told Job that the One who commanded the

morning and the evening had once stood—somewhere in the spans of time—where he now stood: forsaken. His Creator knew what it was like to suffer outside the gates. His Creator knew what it was like to be stripped of everything, to feel shamed. His Creator knew what it was like to be forsaken by not just the world but also by the closest of friends.

The sting of a silent tear rolled down over an open sore on his cheek, reminding him of all he had lost. His children were gone. His home was gone. His possessions were gone. And his friends had done their best to mar the final vestiges of his soul—his integrity.

As the last golden beam pulled its finger from the horizon line, he stood boldly on. His Creator had laid the foundation of the worlds. He knew He had commanded the eagle to mount up and the deer to calve and was the One who gave the raven food for her young. Because of Him, the dawn knew its place, the storehouses of snow were under key, and each constellation would be led forth in its season. His Creator even knew the number of hairs on his head. No longer "in-irons," he felt, for the first time in a long while, a forward progress in his spirit.

Tonight won't be such a lonely, silent night after all, he thought as he stepped down into pathways unseen and rummaged through the dump for an old mat to sleep on and maybe a little something to eat. *God does see me,* spoke his sacrificed heart as he drifted off to sleep in the stench of the city dump. That belief was something this world and its heartache could never strip from him, no matter what table of heartache was set before him.

A Table in the Wilderness

When the harvest gathers more chaff than grain,
And the fig tree produces only thorns;
When poachers drain the last of your honeycomb,
And the well, too, echoes emptiness;
When the wind carries off course the javelin's throw,
And the flowers fade before full bloom;
When the tide erodes your shore of hope,
And difficulties parch your joy;
When the storm refuses to stay at your back,
And reveille turns to taps;
When you're pushed to the brow of the hill
And find no furrow there to catch your footing,
When there is no rock higher than the one you're on,
And life is more a matter of just surviving the day—
Remember that He is able to prepare a table in the
Wilderness and cause manna to rain in the desert;
And may it be there when you need it most that you find
The Bread of Life in abundance!

—Jody

"Then they spoke against God; They said, 'Can God prepare a table in the wilderness?' . . . Yet He commanded the clouds above And opened the doors of heaven; He rained down manna upon them to eat And gave them food from heaven. Man did eat the bread of angels" (Ps. 78:19, 23-25).

10 SPECTACLES OF FAITH

THE HEBREWS 11 HALL OF FAMERS

When skilled masons carefully choose every brick in the pile but you to create their masterpiece, listen for the smoothing sound of the Master's trowel preparing room upon His rejected cornerstone.

—Jody

IT GLOWED HOT RED as he pulled it from the fire. *A good one,* he said to himself as he turned toward the anvil on his workbench and laid the glowing end of the long iron across it. Whistling through his thick beard, he scanned the back wall of his shop for the perfect hammer.

His shop was a basic coppersmith shed. He kept only the important tools of his trade around. He grabbed the hammer and began smiting the hot metal; each stroke was as burly as his own unforgiving frame. Outside, above the doorpost, hung a crude sign with the signature "Alexander the Coppersmith." He was a tough man, a realist, a proud dissenter, and moreover the only coppersmith within miles. So the townspeople had little choice but to go to him with their needs.

"Is my axe ready, Alex?" asked a voice from just outside the door. Alexander didn't look up. He kept smiting the axe head in front of him for a good few minutes. The only sounds to be heard were his heavy rattled breaths. Then he turned with his usual frown and walked toward the barrel of water just outside the doorframe.

"Does it look ready to you?" he barked at the figure on the other side of the steam rising from the barrel. With the metal quenched, he sneered and headed back into his shop. A part of him loved sending people slinking away. It was a game of sorts. Man, woman—it didn't matter. He was in charge of things around here. If they didn't like his unbound gruffness, well, that was just too bad. They would toe tap to him.

Especially that guy Paul. He hated Paul. Just the thought of him made his blood boil. He abhorred his ministry and the teachings he spread of some would-be Messiah.

He laid the quenched metal back on the anvil for shaping and picked up his hammer one more time. Smiting it, he thought of Paul. *If he thinks he's going to spread his teachings 'round these parts, he's got another think coming,* he thought as he slung his temper-driven hammer high above his head and then down toward the anvil. Clink. The undue force split the hammer's handle from end to end in his hand. "Curse you, Paul!" trailed his rebuke through the front doorframe and out through the village. In Paul he had met his match. This was war.

* * *

In 1867 William Seward was rebuked by most everyone. Headlines labeled the United States Secretary of State for both Lincoln's and Johnson's administrations as the biggest fool of all times. "Paper! Paper!" shouted the newsboys through the streets of Virginia. Buggy after buggy clopped along the cobblestone streets before pulling over briefly to retrieve the latest headline news of "Seward's folly." America, under the direction of Secretary of State Seward, had bought what the press harshly portrayed as a "wasteland" from economically struggling Russia.

The chunk of icy land, known today as Alaska, was viewed by most as a worthless piece of land, a foolish purchase by Seward that cost the United States millions—seven, to be exact. Only decades later, with the discovery of gold in its Klondike regions and oil in its wildlife reserves, would "Seward's folly" seem not so foolish after all.

In recent years, Alaska, with its hidden oil reserves, has become a hot button debate. Some view it as our only means for becoming independent from foreign oil. At 2.5 cents per acre, it is perhaps the greatest land purchase of all time. But at the time, William H. Seward was cursed and made a spectacle.

* * *

If you walk this earth for any length of time, you'll eventually come across that gruff Goliath—Alexander Coppersmith. Sometimes he'll come in the form of critical public opinion; other times he comes in the form of a belittling disease. However he comes, his only mission is to oppose and oppose vigorously—especially those who profess their faith in the goodness of God, in heaven—a land unrealized with treasure undiscovered. He hates that kind of people the most. They're "Pauls." They don't mind being fools for a kingdom they've never seen.

The Habakkuk heart is hopeful and can see God's treasures and blessings when no one else can. It walks by faith and not by sight, confident that God is in control, even when the situation of life begs otherwise.

* * *

With her two severely arthritic knees, and a hip injury

that left one leg an inch shorter than the other, she reaches down and gives each barn cat a stroke of affection. "Hey, there, little guy," she whispers before heading up the sidewalk, leaning on her cane. It's 4:30 in the morning. She'll drive five miles to the local high school. Cooking great food and making kids happy is what makes her happy. After adopting and raising five now-grown kids, her mission in life hasn't much changed: loving kids. *Lord, the kids would love it if we purchased that new slushy machine*, she prayed as she drove. Her five-mile drive to the school had become five miles of prayers. In that short stretch of country road, she covered her family, her kids, her grandkids, the relatives, friends, and the neighbors. Calling them by name, she asked God to protect them physically, mentally, emotionally, and spiritually.

With heavy doses she prayed for her teenage grandsons. She knew they were at a stage in life where they needed to learn to make good choices, just like the teenagers she served each day. *Please use me today at school,* came her final prayer as she pulled to the curb of Colfax High School. Walking in, she greeted everyone with her usual smile. No one ever noticed her cane much—just her smile.

A trip to the cafeteria meant you would get not only great food but it would also be served with smiles. More than 400 students walked through her lunchroom each day, and she made a point to get to know each one as an individual. The teenagers who worked back in the kitchen with her received unexpected presents on their birthdays or for Christmas. She found out their interests and then gave a shirt from a hip clothing store or a gift certificate to a place that meant a lot to them. She kept an eye on the athletes as they went through and made sure they felt full for their upcoming games.

"Are you ready for the big game?" she would say as she heaped an extra helping onto the plate. Every kid mattered, the troubled kids especially. She kept a close eye on the kids "falling through the cracks." Disarmed by her humor, they trusted her enough to open up sometimes. Some without homes and families of their own would end up in her home as a foster kid. She could see buried treasure in each of them, and as she cooked and fed them, she panned for that gold.

Her knees and hip gave her fits most every day. But no one ever knew. She pushed her lunch cart around not only to serve others but also to lean on in getting around. At the close of each day she parked her cart, hung up her apron, and drove her five miles of prayer back home.

Her Habakkuk heart was relentless. She didn't have time to think about her own limp, about how Alexander the Coppersmith was trying to smite her health. She had other things to think about: 400 kids and their needs. Her heart was where her treasure was, and her treasure was in serving those kids in every way and any way imaginable.

Thank you, Lord, for the slushy machine that will be coming tomorrow. The kids will love it! I think I'll order berry, cherry, and lime flavors. It might be nice to take some of the first samples down to the secretary first thing in the morning, she prayed as she continued her five miles of prayers for others. Her arthritic knees, healing shoulder, and hip injury never made the headlines of her prayers. Her Habakkuk heart was too busy praying others through their days. *And maybe the kids can play some of their music in the cafeteria at lunch.*

I don't know how Alexander the Coppersmith has smote you lately. Maybe you're dealing with a debilitating illness. You may feel that you've been forged beyond what you're able to handle and that you've been heated up and dunked under for quenching and then heated back up again and again. You're probably out of breath and weary from it all. A coppersmith has hold of you.

But there's another coppersmith besides Alexander. And in His hands your Habakkuk heart will be refined to the point that no one will notice your limp. Regardless of your battle, the good Coppersmith can take what Alexander meant for evil and forge in you a Habakkuk heart so buoyant that nothing will keep you down.

* * *

He lay there bleeding. It surprised him how calm he was. He knew his folks would be home soon. They rarely ever left him alone these days, because his seizures were flaring up. He was glad they had been able to get away for a few hours. He reached his hand up and felt the back of his head. A heavy flow of blood dripped down around his neck. *I hope this doesn't stain the carpet,* he thought as he lay there.

The muscular disease that many doctors had no name for made walking or standing difficult. At 20-something, he had spent the last few years slowly losing his ability to walk or move inch by inch. At first he was able to get around with a lumbering gait; then he needed a cane to steady himself, then a walker, and more recently he needed a motorized chair to get around.

Lying there, he thought of his dog. They had become good buds. He thought of his horse, Sarah. She was the perfect horse. With one side of his face to the floor, he scanned the top of the carpet's plush pile. *I really hope I'm not making a mess.* He stretched his right arm out toward the wheelchair. Maybe he could grab it and drag it closer. He stretched as far as he could. It was no use—it was out of reach.

Dropping his hand flat to the floor, he stroked the carpet. It was soft, just like Sarah's muzzle. He loved to feed Sarah. All he had to do was stretch the flat of his palm through the barbwire fence and wait for her to come. She always did. Her soft muzzle gingerly nibbled at the carrot in his hand as he stroked her mane. He continued stroking the carpet. Riding Sarah gave him mobility and freedom. In a way, she made him feel whole again. *Thank you for Sarah, Lord.*

With his other hand, he felt the back of his head again; the blood was coming a bit more profusely now.

Viewing his bloodied fingertips made him a little queasy. He closed his eyes. *Blood.* He thought of the church songs he sang as a little kid. He had gone to every summer Bible School since he was six, and as he got older he helped serve the counselors and even played his guitar for the campers. Those songs were ingrained into his head. He could sing them in his sleep.

He felt the back of his head with his hand one more time. Blood covered his whole hand this time. He closed his eyes again. *My heart was dark with sin, until the Savior came in, His precious blood I know has washed me white as snow; and in God's Word I'm told, I'll walk the streets of gold.* (by Frances J. Roberts, "Wordless Book Song," © 1974 Child Evangelism Fellowship, Inc. Used by permission.) Walk. *Someday,* he thought. Someday he would walk the way he used to and get around the way he used to and go as fast as he wanted to wherever he wanted. *Cool.* He wouldn't have to use his walker to go down the aisle for communion. He could use his legs. *That would be the bomb, Lord,* prayed his youthful heart.

And so were the musings of Jason's Habakkuk heart as he lay there bleeding.

His parents came through the front door to find Jason had nearly bled to death. The gash in his head had sliced to his skull. It required three layers of stitches. But Jason's Habakkuk heart couldn't be suppressed. He was in church the following Sunday, praising God, never knowing if the next seizure would hit before he finished the song.

* * *

This summer a bird made her nest in the corner of the eave out our back door down along the farthest corner of the deck. The homeowner in me says I should have cleared it out a month ago. But I didn't. Now that mother bird perches there morning, noon, and night to feed these fuzzy heads with gaping beaks. That's all you can see of them as they pop above the eave. I can't knock the nest down—not now. It's alive. So, I'll just spend my noontime watching them. What's striking is that as soon as that mother bird barely rustles the edge of the eave, pinkish-red beaks pop wide open and remain open until she feeds them. Sometimes she feeds them, and sometimes she just sits with them. Funny. The little beaks remain wide open even when she's just there to sit with them. She knows what they need and when they need it.

We're all like that with our Creator. We keep our beaks gaping wide, ready for blessings and favor and anything else wonderful that He might drop into our lives. And our appetites are ferocious. It's a wonder He doesn't get tired of us. We often treat Him as if He exists only to feed us. *Where's my blessing, Lord? Where's my healing, Lord? Where's my wealth, Lord? Where's my protection, Lord? Where's my harvest, Lord? I've been laboring for you!* Chirp, chirp, chirp. One demanding chirp after another after another.

But when God perches at the edge of the Habakkuk heart, it's a whole other story. The Habakkuk heart enjoys just the presence of God. The Habakkuk heart doesn't sit with its beak open—it's just as satisfied when no worm is thrown into its nest as when a worm is thrown in. It has no demands; it worries more about the carpet than bleeding to death. It's the kind of heart that limps to work so it can heal the hurting places in a teenager's heart. It's the kind of heart that arrests the heavens and causes angels to draw near, for it is never fuller than when the One who loves it comes and sits just to be near.

* * *

A pair of old canvas running shoes—you saw them as soon as you walked through the door. They made it impossible to keep that lump from welling up in your throat. Those shoes had run all over town and right into the hearts of the community. Today they're displayed on a table in the narthex of the largest church in town. With the passing of the yellow blooms that fall, Karyn is gone. The walls were bursting at the seams as an unending flow of people streamed through the doors to pay their last respects.

She was in her 30s, a petite blonde. Well, all of her was petite except for her larger-than-life smile. She could say everything with that big, welcoming grin. You really felt "liked" when she flashed it at you. She loved her woman's Bible study group, her kids, and her friends. She had a quirky shoe fetish that was endearing. She was so accessible. Could she really be gone? No one held the sling of faith higher nor flung the rock of courage farther than

Karyn. *Cancer, you Goliath, didn't you know her Habakkuk heart would have the last word?*

A month earlier she had laid her head back in the chair and let the chemo drip through her I.V. She envisioned wild horses running through a valley, their manes dancing in the wind as they tromped across rattlesnakes slithering through the grasses. To her, cancer represented those rattlesnakes, and the chemo treatment running through her body was the horses. She used her mind and anything else God gave her to battle this Goliath. *Thank you, Jesus, for getting me through one more treatment,* she prayed as they unhooked her from her chemotherapy session. She knew He had been by her side and ridden wild horses with her, stampeding the enemy.

Cancer should have sunk her several times. But she fought a good 10 years against it—enough years to make a difference in the lives of her teenage kids, Marcus and Karley, and to pass on to them her courageous faith. Her faith was strong and sharp and sure and absolutely irrepressible. Like a buoyant axe head, it didn't matter how far cancer tried to quench her faith—she kept bobbing up to the surface.

I Can Do All Things Through Christ Who Strengthens Me read the sign above her kitchen sink. Whether at chemo or out following her kids to their sporting events, she sensed the rustling presence of God at her side, giving her strength and assurance. As she threw on her tennis shoes each day for a run, she heard the wild horses running and stomping out the rattlesnakes before her. In the distance, the handle of a hammer split from end to end. It belonged to a certain coppersmith. In Karyn he had met his match. This was war.

* * *

During World War II, allies were scrambling to invent new and unique weapons. Some ideas included incendiary devices that could be strapped to bats. Many ideas were pursued, but none were as large in scale as the aircraft carrier *Habakkuk*. It was the brainchild of Geoffrey Pyke, who convinced Churchill that a floating "ice ship" could withstand the Nazi torpedoes from German U-boats. Since steel had become a shrinking commodity during the war, an iceberg-type aircraft carrier seemed like the ticket. It would be both buoyant and strong and sturdy enough to take a few hits. It would house an airstrip, numerous antiaircraft guns, and up to 150 twin-engine bombers or fighters.

A small model of the idea was built. There was one problem: the frozen blocks of ice that were used weren't as strong as a glacier. Geoffrey Pyke set to work and came up with a way to make the ice stronger. By the addition of 13-percent cellulose in the form of sawdust, wood chips, and paper shreds, the ice was stronger. It seemed the ship might be built after all.

However, the unsinkable *Habakkuk* made it no farther than the design table. The amount of wood pulp Pyke needed to build it would impact paper production and prove to be too costly. Pyke's dream of a ship that would live up to the biblical book for which it was named never materialized. "Be utterly amazed, for I am going to do something in your days that you would not believe, even if you were told" (Hab. 1:5).

Habakkuk was never built. It would have been the strongest ship ever. Its solid buoyancy would have wearied the enemy. What people didn't build, however, God did build. God's floating iron is the Habakkuk heart. Its irrepressible hope beats in no other.

> Now the sons of the prophets said to Elisha, "Behold now, the place before you where we are living is too limited for us. Please let us go to the Jordan and each of us take from there a beam, and let us make a place there for ourselves where we may live." So he said, "Go." Then one said, "Please be willing to go with your servants." And he answered, "I shall go." So he went with them; and when they came to the Jordan, they cut down trees. But as one was felling a beam, the axe head fell into the water; and he cried out and said, "Alas, my master! For it was borrowed." Then the man of God said, "Where did it fall?" And when he showed him the place, he cut off a stick and threw it in there, and made the iron float. He said, "Take it up for yourself." So he put out his hand and took it *(2 Kings 6:1-7).*

What makes iron float? What makes the Habakkuk heart so buoyant? Its purposes in life are to honor God and honor people—in that order. It's a heart that isn't bitter about its circumstances, because it knows without a doubt that there is a plan and that there is a Creator who can make all things work together for good. It keeps trusting. It keeps hoping. Whether working in a cafeteria with a limp, lying in a pool of blood with a gash to the head, or hooked up to chemotherapy treatments, this heart keeps an eternal perspective. It keeps smiling. It keeps singing in church. Its buoyancy wearies the enemy.

How do we keep an eternal perspective in the midst of suffering? How can we have hearts of floating iron? How can we remain strong and sure and hopeful in sinking circumstances?

* * *

The Four Ts of the Habakkuk Heart

Transparency: The Habakkuk heart runs to God and pours out its concern with candor and honesty.

Time: The Habakkuk heart spends time in silence, listening for God's response, waiting for peace that surpasses understanding.

Thanksgiving: The Habakkuk heart sees God's goodness and gives thanks in all circumstances.

Trust: The Habakkuk heart trusts God even when the evidence of life begs otherwise.

* * *

It was dusk. He made his way out of the village through a valley where a herd of cattle grazed. Up a sloping hill he climbed. The tall grasses lapped at his calves. As he walked, he thought about the impending doom. A few outcroppings of rocks detoured him up and around until he reached the plateau at the top. Out of breath, he stopped. He could see miles in every direction. A few yards away was a building where many of the prophets, himself included, used to get away from it all and pray.

He stood and watched the sun sink below the horizon, its warm glow melting into the crest of the Judean hillsides. There was solace here that he couldn't find anywhere else. He pulled a long piece of grass and put it to his mouth. It was bitter. Chewing it, he stood gazing at the sunset. The Chaldeans were coming. That much he knew. It was the talk of the town among the panicked villagers who were preparing for the fierce and impetuous people. The Chaldeans were an enemy unlike any other. They seized dwelling places that were not theirs. Their horses were swifter than leopards and keener than wolves.

Chewing on the piece of grass, Habakkuk disappeared into the building. Just inside the door, he grabbed one of the stone tablets to log his daily prayer. All the prophets used them. Around and around he climbed the towering steps with the tablet tucked under one arm and the long grass still in his mouth. "How long, O Lord, will I call for help, and You will not hear? I cry out to you, 'Violence!' Yet You do not save" (Hab. 1:2).

He stopped and looked out a tall rectangular window inside the brick tower about halfway up and peered out at his village below. He lived in a land governed by crooked men. Laws were ignored; wickedness was served, so justice always came out perverted.

"Why do you make me see iniquity, And cause me to look on wickedness?" Habakkuk prayed out loud (Hab. 1:3) as he peered through the window and listened for God's reply.

"I am doing something in your day you would not believe if you were told. I am raising up that impetuous people, the Chaldeans. They will make the perverted rulers of your land a laughing matter," said God.

Habakkuk continued up the stairs. He wondered what God was up to. When he reached the top, he looked out over the rampart. Up there he could get his bearings. Things seemed clearer at the top of the watchtower. He slipped through a small doorway onto a deck of sorts. The night sky engulfed him. The stars were twinkling overhead and a slight southerly wind swept gently through the tall grasses. He put his tablet aside and looked out over the landscape, pressing his lips to the piece of grass. He was troubled. How could the Lord use that wicked, impetuous people, the Chaldeans, to chasten the waywardness of his people? It seemed unfair.

He pulled the grass from his mouth and flung it angrily over the waist-high rock wall. "Why do You look with favor on those who deal treacherously? Why are you silent when the wicked swallow up those who are more righteous then they?" Habakkuk asked sternly.

A gentle wind circled the stone tower, the tall grasses at the base swayed in unison, a lock of Habakkuk's thick hair swept down over his eyes. He couldn't see. He felt confused about the God he served.

"Record the vision," answered the Lord through the breeze. Habakkuk's heart quickened as he pulled the tablet onto his lap and began writing. "I have a plan, Habakkuk. It hastens toward a goal and will not fail. Though it tarries, wait for it."

Habakkuk sat and wrote: "Behold, as for the proud one, His soul is not right within him; but the righteous will live by faith." Habakkuk's heart sank. He reached up and pulled the lock of hair from his eyes and looked out over the land. He knew his God wanted him to walk by faith and not by sight. But his sight told him his country was a mess. His sight told him it was hopeless. Self-serving men ruled his land. He picked his pen up again. "Woe to him who gets evil gain for his house to put his nest on high." So continued the Lord's woes through Habakkuk's pen all through the night.

It was nearly daybreak when he set the tablet aside. God had reminded him of His faithfulness in the past: how He had sent the plagues, how He had parted the Red Sea, and all the other wondrous works of His hands. Habakkuk's heart felt renewed. He knew God would not let injustice go. He knew his God to be a fair God and that in His time everything would work out. In His time.

He grabbed the tablet and started back down the winding stairwell. Halfway down, he paused and looked out the tall, rectangular window. *I know you have a plan, Lord. I know you're still on the throne. The mountains see you and quake. The sun and moon stand in their places,* he prayed as he looked out the window. He squinted at the morning sun slicing through the horizon. "His radiance is like the sunlight; He has rays flashing from His hand, And there is the hiding of His power," spoke the Lord to Habakkuk's heart (Hab. 3:4). He continued down the stairwell. Each step echoed hope. He knew God was in control. He thought about how "the hiding of His power" was in His hand. Though he couldn't imagine fully what that meant, he sensed it had something to do with the promise of the coming Messiah. *Surely there would be power in His hands.*

He reached the last step and headed out into the morning sun. Down the hill the tall grasses lapped at his calves. He plucked a tall piece as he walked and pressed it between his lips. It seemed sweeter this time. Having poured his concerns before the Lord, he found his heart filled with peaceful confidence as he walked. He knew the Chaldeans would sweep through and pilfer his land and his people and their property in the coming hours. Yet his inward man sipped on the sweetness of the night watch. "Though the fig tree should not blossom And there be no fruit on the vines . . . And there be no cattle in the stalls, Yet I will exult in the LORD" (Hab. 3:17-18). Down the hill and around the outcroppings of rocks he made his way to the floor of the green valley below. The cattle were gone—

a sure sign the Chaldeans were coming. "Yet I will exult in the LORD," said Habakkuk's heart.

* * *

An empty nursery, the broken body of a faithful chaplain, a precious life lost to cancer, a young man living with the reality of day-to-day seizures—life is hard.

Sometimes Goliath doesn't fall.

It has nothing to do with how much or little faith you have and everything to do with the fact that we live in a fallen world, a world where the original sin of the garden unlocked the dungeon door and where ruthless giants now roam and play havoc in our lives. Like Alexander the coppersmith, they want to do you much harm.

It's when Goliath doesn't fall, however, that you'll come fact to face with the One who wasn't delivered from the sting of life's whip either. If you let Him, He will meet you on the outer banks of suffering and give you a different kind of deliverance. In His nail-pierced hands is a hiding of power that will wipe away your tears and carry you through. He'll be with you to the end, just as He was with all the Habakkuk hearts that have gone before you. In this world they didn't receive prosperity or deliverance but, in fact, just the opposite. And yet their hearts remained rich toward God.

Mathew was killed by the sword.

Mark was dragged by horses through the streets until he died.

Luke was hanged.

Peter was crucified upside down.

James, a brother of Jesus, was thrown down more than a hundred feet from the southeast pinnacle of the Temple.

James, the son of Zebedee, was beheaded, but not before a Roman soldier witnessed his courage and knelt beside him to accept beheading also, as a Christian.

Bartholomew was whipped to death.

Thomas was speared.

Jude was killed with arrows.

Barnabas was stoned to death.

John the Baptist was beheaded.

Paul was tortured and then beheaded by Nero in A.D. 67.

Other Christians were made to wear wax shirts and set on fire to light Nero's gardens.

The Habakkuk heart offers a different sort of worship—not the old prosperity-or-bust kind of worship, but an unconditional and strangely hopeful worship, a courageously wild worship that exalts the Lord even when there is no fruit on the vine and no cattle in the stalls. It's a heart that sets itself apart from the rest, for it's a heart that worships the one true God of the Bible in the middle of suffering. It's a heart that captures the heart of God, enthralling Him to its side.

Only a Habakkuk heart could sit in a pew the Sunday morning after burying a son. Only the Habakkuk heart could offer up songs knowing the next seizure could hit before the song is over. Only the Habakkuk heart would smile at cancer and dare it to keep up! Only the Habakkuk heart would endure being heated to a red glow. Only the Habakkuk heart would be made a spectacle for its faith.

The Spectacles of Faith

Faith builds a ship in the desert—and saves humanity.
Faith worships while leaning atop a staff—and a nation is blessed.
Faith hides its treasure in a basket of reeds—and delivers a prince who delivers a people.
Faith speaks not a word as it marches day after day—and with a shout a city falls.
Faith risks its life to protect two messengers of God—and survives judgment.
Faith grabs an empty pitcher—and defeats an army.
Faith picks up a pebble—and slays a giant.
Faith enters the lion's den and the heat of the furnace—and kings bow.
Faith steps out of the boat and into the storm—and God builds a church upon it.
Faith sings with its wrists bound in chains—and the earth quakes.

Called is the pilgrim to wear the spectacles of faith, which he will put into the drawer when he arrives home. Until then, they're worn so that he might peer into space and time and enjoy the starry host from a distance.

—Jody

> Through faith [they] subdued kingdoms, wrought righteousness, obtained promises, stopped the mouths

of lions. Quenched the violence of fire, escaped the edge of the sword, out of weakness were made strong, waxed valiant in fight, turned to flight the armies of the aliens. Women received their dead raised to life again: and others were tortured, not accepting deliverance; that they might obtain a better resurrection: And others had trial of cruel mockings and scourgings, yea, moreover of bonds and imprisonment: They were stoned, they were sawn asunder, were tempted, were slain with the sword: they wandered about in sheepskins and goatskins; being destitute, afflicted, tormented; (Of whom the world was not worthy:) they wandered in deserts, and in mountains, and in dens and caves of the earth *(Heb. 11:33-38, KJV)*.

11
IN DOMINO FASHION

THE HOPE OF THE HABAKKUK HEART

Intertwined lives is the Body of Christ,
Sinews of faith;
Stretched ready to race a relay of God's grace.
—Jody

THERE'S SOMETHING ABOUT a football game under the lights on a Friday night. My teenage son says it's the ultimate. "I can't explain it, Mom. It's a fight—it's like being a gladiator out there for the whole town, and they're behind you, cheering, saying 'Our town is the best!'"

That's the way my son sees it. While I'm tempted to get out my flower-printed ironing board and straighten out his perception of being a beast on the field with my own "pretty" ideas about faith, I realize he's more on the mark about living out this thing called faith than a lot of churchgoers, me included. Many Christians have turned the gladiator love of Christ, who fought the darkness of the underworld and wouldn't stop until He reached the goal line of winning our souls back, into a pretty, let's-sit-down-in-the-grass-and-pick-daisies kind of faith.

Life is hard. Sometimes no matter how hard we pray, babies do die. Sometimes no matter how loyal we've been, the world abandons us. And more times than not, nice guys *do* finish last. In this world of suffering and underhanded blows from roaming Goliaths, we need more than the "pretty" Jesus created by religious do-gooders. We need a gladiator Jesus who has walked ahead of us. We need a Savior who will come alongside and help us when Goliath gets away with a clip—when Goliath doesn't fall.

That's the Savior we need. And that's the Savior we have. Some 2,000 years ago, Jesus Christ ran a dangerous gridiron gauntlet to call us His own and was battered the whole 100 yards. He never stopped. He never quit. Bloodied and beaten, He kept getting up. He calls us into a wild faith that follows Him toward the goal. It's not what happens at the scrimmage line that counts—it's what happens as we follow Him triumphantly into the end zone ahead.

From the ashes of the Holocaust, which claimed the lives of millions of Jews, the nation of Israel was birthed.

"It's hard to believe that from something so horrific could come good," noted our pastor one Sunday morning, referring to the Holocaust. "But God did trump evil and cause good to come of it."

Only God could take a Goliath as big and ugly as the Holocaust, with its smug look of victory, and work it together for good. The Goliath of the Holocaust did eventually fall. And from its ashes Israel rose. It's just as He said it would be, as He said thousands of years ago. Four thousand years ago, to be precise.

Consider the story of Jacob, taken from chapters 28 and 29 of the Book of Genesis. As a 17-year-old boy, he was sent away with his father's blessings and told to go to Paddan-aran, where his mother's relatives lived and where he was to take a wife. After traveling some 70 miles, the young lad was tired and laid down to rest. *A little shut-eye will renew me*, he thought as he scanned the scrub brush for a flat rock. Using the rock for a pillow, he kept his head out of the hot sand and soon fell asleep. Then came the dream.

In his dream a ladder descended from the clouds. One end sat on earth and the other in heaven. Angels of God were ascending and descending on it.

The LORD stood above it and said, "I am the LORD, the God of your father Abraham and the God of Isaac; the land on which you lie, I will give it to you and to your descendants. Your descendants will also be like the dust of the earth, and you will spread out to the west and to the east and to the north and to the south; and in you and in your descendants shall all the families of the earth be blessed. Behold, I am with you and will keep you wherever you go, and will bring you back to this land; for I will not leave you until I have done what I have promised you" (*Gen. 28:13-15*).

Jacob woke and said, "'How awesome is this place! This is none other than the house of God, and this is the gate of heaven.' So Jacob rose early in the morning, and took the stone that he had put under his head and set it up as a pillar and poured oil on its top. He called the name of that place Bethel" (vv. 17-19).

Then he continued on his journey. He hadn't gone far when up ahead he saw sheep bedded down near a well waiting to be watered. A few shepherds stood guard as they waited for other shepherds to come in with their flocks. Together they would be able to move the stone from the top of the well that sealed the water and kept it fresh. Jacob approached the shepherds and said, "Hello, where are you from?"

"We're from Haran," they said

"Do you know Laban son of Hahor?"

"Why, yes!" they replied.

"Does he live far from here?" inquired Jacob.

"Ask his daughter, Rachel. There she is coming in with the flock for watering." Jacob raised his hand over his brow and peered at the hazy figure making its way across the fields.

"What's her name again?" he asked.

"Rachel." They replied. "She's a local shepherdess."

Jacob watched as she made her way in. He was intrigued. Even in the distance, her emerging form was captivating. He wondered if she was a mirage. The clamoring and greeting from other shepherds arriving to help remove the rock that capped the well flooded his hearing like distant white noise. All of his attention was focused on the figure in the distance moving toward them. For a moment she sank from his sight as she and the sheep she was guiding dipped into a shallow knoll.

He held his breath.

As the gnarly top of her staff bobbed back into sight, he strained for a better look at her in the desert sun. First the top of her head appeared. Long chestnut hair poured out from under a modest head dress, draping out around her delicate neck. Then the rest of her appeared. Jacob watched as she gently guided a little lamb in behind the rest of the flock. Soon the bleating of sheep circled his feet along with a thin cloud of dust. He blinked but never moved his gaze from Rachel, who was just yards from him.

Her skin was beautiful. Her large doe eyes lifted toward his. She gracefully wiped her brow. His heart raced. He knew she had come for water. Without thinking, he rushed to her aid and lifted the heavy stone away from the well all by himself. At that moment he knew that he would do anything for her. He leaned in and greeted her with a kiss. Her beauty made him cry.

Jacob would work seven long years for Rachel's hand. When those seven years were behind him, his greedy father-in-law, Laban, tricked him into marrying his other daughter, Leah. To have Rachel's hand, Jacob had to work another seven years. However, "they seemed to him but a few days because of his love for her" (v. 20).

When was the last time your labor for the Lord seemed like only a few days? Laboring in Christ can mean a lot of things. It most likely includes suffering. Every day, Jacob labored under the sun in unpleasant conditions. He sat through rainstorms and watched over the flocks through the night. He probably got cold sitting out there passing his time. He probably got overheated. But his pain and toil seemed but a few days because of his love for Rachel.

Are you feeling as if your labor for the Lord is in vain? Maybe you've been battered around on the gridiron for many years. Remember the Habakkuk perspective. Keep your eye on the end zone ahead of you.

"Whatever is true, whatever is noble, whatever is right, whatever is pure, whatever is lovely, whatever is admirable—if anything is excellent or praiseworthy—think about such things" (Phil. 4:8, NIV).

After years of labor, Jacob married his love, Rachel. He had set his mind on her throughout all his days and years of toil. She was what kept him going. Just the thought of her kept him shearing the sheep in the hot sun and enduring the long cold nights. He knew God had blessed him just as he said He would in his dream. After years of Jacob's wrestling for blessing, God gave him the name "Israel." Rachel gave birth to two sons: Joseph, who later became second in command of Egypt; and another son, Benjamin. Altogether, Rachel and Leah gave Jacob 12 sons, who became the 12 tribes of Israel, which later became the nation of Israel.

* * *

The gymnasium was packed to overflowing. It was both a hometown crowd and an out-of-town crowd. Many had traveled in from around the country. The "Bryan Golden Bears" logo emblazoned across the wall of the gym had never hung above such a large crowd.

He sat in the front row of folding chairs and looked down at his hands. He was burying his boy today. *I know you can make something good come from this,* he prayed to his God as he dealt with the feeling of having his legs ripped out from under him. It was hard to believe how drastic life had changed in a matter of days. Again and again, he ran the edge of his shirt through his thumb and forefinger and thought about how only a few days earlier he was traveling to Fort Myers, Florida, to see his son play in a spring baseball tournament. *Oh, how I loved to watch that kid play!* he thought, smiling through tears.

His tears fell along the hem of the shirt he wore. It had been his son's shirt, his baseball jersey.

Thousands had turned out for David Betts's funeral. The young man with the smile of adventure and a heart for everyone he met had obviously touched a lot of lives. A gifted athlete, David had been humble about the talent that made him the starting sophomore infielder for Bluffton University's baseball team. He had been a likeable kid. He loved his family and had looked up to his older sister, who shared his love for baseball. He wanted to be like her in a lot of ways and maybe even set a few records in baseball the way she had in her college softball career. They were close. Now he was gone.

His close-knit ties extended beyond his immediate family to the campus of Bluffton University. Those people were his family too. They had shared the most intimate aspect of his life—his deep faith in a just and holy God.

"Where was this just God the day this all happened?" asked the smug, roaming giants hidden among the headlines of newspapers across the nation. How does a bus plunge off a highway overpass?

It was reported that the bus driver had been well rested the night of the accident. His wife, in the front seat near him, even offered another pair of eyes for the journey. So how did it happen that a bus would take an exit ramp and never apply the brakes for the stop sign at the top of the overpass, but instead go through the stop sign, cross two lanes, plow through a concrete barrier, and plunge some 30 feet to the highway below?

Many conjecture that the Ohio driver probably didn't realize he was even on an exit ramp. More than likely, he probably thought that night that his commuter bus was a mile farther up the road where the highway does follow a natural bend. It was a mistake even experienced Atlanta drivers admit to making due to Atlanta's extraordinarily convoluted highways and byways.

"The road was coming up after me," a surviving baseball player later reported. Six of his buddies did not survive. Another eight were hospitalized for injuries. The impact of the bus left shattered glass and baseball paraphernalia sprawled across the highway. Atlanta first responders called the accident site "catastrophic."

Parents hopped planes and rushed to Atlanta. Some found their sons beat up but alive at an area hospital. Others would not be so lucky.

David Betts's father was on route to Sarasota, Florida, for his son's opening game when he got the call.

Back to Atlanta? The game is in Florida, he reasoned. Grasping in pieces what had taken place, he ran to the airport to catch the next available flight. The accident sounded bad. A large chartered bus doesn't fall some 30 feet from an overpass without creating a lot of damage. He wondered what kind of damage. He hoped for the best as he prayed the whole plane ride. As soon as his feet hit Atlanta soil, however, he learned the news.

As other parents rushed to the hospital, David Betts's father was led to the morgue. Gulping down a lifetime of memories and love for his boy, he made the positive identification.

A CNN television report would recount what David Betts's father did. He didn't go home and try to catch his breath from the shock and horror of losing his son. No. Instead, he headed to the county hospital. *What for?* viewers wondered. *His son was dead.*

"Those boys needed to be comforted," John Betts said to the listening and watching world as reporters retraced his rush to the hospital, where he embraced each boy. "They needed to know this hasn't all happened for no good reason. Something good will come of this." With the cameras rolling, players on the Bluffton baseball team shared their views of this father and how his love for them in the midst of his own private grief helped them heal and recover from their injuries and the emotions of survivor's guilt.

What kind of heart, in the midst of its own unspeakable grief, rushes from identifying his son at the morgue to the hospital where someone else's son lay intact? Only a Habakkuk with a gladiator faith could get up and rush a few more yards after taking such a Goliath hit.

This father's Habakkuk heart believed in a just and holy God while standing in the most unjust and unholy moment of his life. "Something good will come of this." His words reverberated, smacking a blow to the lurking Goliaths at large. Under the brim of a baseball cap, this father's tear-filled eyes spoke confidence in an almighty God.

God didn't create this fallen world—sin did. The Holocaust wasn't His idea nor was a bus plunging off an overpass. God is good. God is holy. No evil is found in Him.

No evil comes from Him. When a Goliath enters our lives, it can cause us to wonder who's in control. But rest assured that in the grand scheme of things—in the broader expanse of time—Goliath's allotted hour is short.

God is in control. He can cause a nation to rise from ashes. He can cause hope to rise from a highway catastrophe. He sees you. And He sees your suffering. It hurts Him to see you going through what you're going through.

The Heavenly Father grieved the day His Son did not survive the plunge. Two thousand years ago, His Son plunged from the royalties of heaven to earth, where He wore a crown of thorns. As His Son lay in Golgotha's morgue with a broken heart, the Heavenly Father's thoughts turned to us. "For God so loved the world, that He gave His only begotten Son" (John 3:16).

The Heavenly Father has already walked through the valley you now face. With a silent tear, He watched His Son suffer on the Cross that Friday. In His sovereignty He vowed that something good would come of this. And something did: humanity's redemption, humanity's second chance to reverse the curse of the garden and once again have an intimate relationship with God.

Few would follow into battle a leader with no battle scars of experience. Our God conquered death and the grave, and He has the scars to prove it. He's the most qualified leader. We need Him, a leader who can show us how to live out a gladiator faith, who can transform our hearts into Habakkuk hearts so that we can see hope in the midst of hopelessness, a leader who can get us through the deepest of valleys. There's only One who has walked those kinds of cliffs with success—Jesus Christ. He rose from Golgotha—and promises to raise you from your Golgotha.

In Bryan, Ohio, lives a man with a Habakkuk heart. He'll never see his son play another baseball game, yet he lives his days with hope and continues to cheer for the Bluffton University baseball team. His Habakkuk heart arrests the heavens. In no other worship is there found a more poignant note of praise than the Habakkuk heart, for it offers worship in the face of a menacing Goliath.

Whether there's fruit on the vine or cattle in the stalls or not, whether his son lay in a hospital bed or a morgue, this Habakkuk heart exalts the Lord and gives the world a look into the wonder of a God who inspires such devotion. John Betts's Habakkuk heart knows God has walked before him and has secured a destiny in heaven.

* * *

Friday night under the lights is special in our hometown. Families fill the bleachers and bundle under blankets. The smell of popcorn fills the air, and anticipation builds with each note of the band. It's game time. You can feel the town pride swell as our guys run onto the field in their blue and gold uniforms. It's time to face off with some giants. The crowd stands as the gladiator hearts on the gridiron below get ready to go head to head. For four solid quarters they never quit. They give it their all and keep pushing forward, and that's what makes our little town glad.

Perhaps as it is on earth so it is in heaven. Maybe all the Habakkuk hearts down through the ages who have suffered through staggering losses such as cancer, slander, misrepresentation, hurricanes, disease, hardship, persecution, the loss of a child, the loss of dreams—maybe all the tears from all the believers who kept getting up and running and praising God even when Goliath didn't fall are tears kept by God.

John 4:14 says that inside every believing heart there is "a well of water springing up to eternal life." From the same Spirit-filled well flow the tears of believers in Christ. In no other tears is there found a more poignant note of praise than in the tears of a wounded worshiper.

How that praise must sound in heaven—the sound of praise that comes not from someone who's been healed or delivered from certain death but from someone who *hasn't*! It's unconditional praise and unconditional worship. It comes from a Habakkuk heart.

How that praise must sound in hell! You can almost hear darkness pout. The sound of such rare praise puts darkness on notice and causes cursing in the enemy's camp.

No matter how dire the situation, the Habakkuk heart praises its Maker unconditionally.

On this side of heaven we don't know exactly what the city of God looks like. It's described as one that glitters more brightly than any other city you can think of and one that will be full of activity and purpose and beauty. A river runs through it "whose streams make glad the city of God" (Ps. 46:4). Maybe every faith-filled tear from every believer down through the ages will mingle into a river of faith that will make glad the city of God.

In our local football games our boys get up tackle after tackle, because they know the end zone is ahead of them just beyond the line of Goliaths. They know that when they reach the end zone, an entire city will erupt in cheer and be glad.

Have you slung the rock of faith only to look up and find Goliath still standing with that same smug look on his face? Keep trusting. Keep getting up. Keep the gladiator faith of the Habakkuk heart, which knows that God is lining up somewhere down the field and that your Goliath will fall and cause other Goliaths behind him to fall in domino fashion. Perhaps your gladiator faith will inspire others and make glad entire cities—maybe even the city of God.

A River of Faith

From a servant quarter's waning wall
ballet earth-touched prayers into celestial halls,
where tears of mingling expanses resign on toe
before the waxing heart of Royalty's throne
From where one day shall spill
a waterfall of blessing alongside heaven's city-streamed-streets, a bottled flow of faith-filled tears from persecuted saints throughout the years, a river of faith making glad God's most holy dwelling place.

—Jody

12
IN DEFIANCE
KNOWING THE DISTANCE HE RAN FOR YOU

When it seems sin reigns sovereign and the pathway's stumbling dark, cutting through the night to shine stark white is the Lily of the Valley, aiding travelers to walk by faith and not by sight.

—Jody

"IT'S GETTING DARK!" yelled a player. "Let's head back to our dorm rooms."

"No pain, no glory!" Liz snipped as she side-stepped a defender and dribbled a few more yards up field. With her wad of gum clenched between her teeth and her cheeks aglow from the fall night, she took aim, swung her leg with all her might, and sent the ball sailing across the field to a fellow teammate poised and readied to swoop it into the net.

"Score!" she hollered as she thrust her fists into the darkness and waited for the rest of her teammates to catch up with her on the moonlit field.

"It's just a friendly pick-up game, Liz. Boy—you'd think you won some sort of championship or something," chided her friends lagging up to give her a pat on the back.

But to Liz Duncan every moment was worth a championship effort. That's how she played the game of soccer. That's how she played the game of life—all out, full tilt, no holding back. The evidence was everywhere. Whether studying biology late into the night or working at her part-time job at McDonald's or just studying her Bible at the local coffee shop, Liz lived up to advice on the sticky note above her computer screen: LIFE'S SHORT. RUN LONG.

"Can I get you a refill?" she said to the man alone in the corner booth as she stood to refill her own cup from the self-serve coffee pot in the corner.

"No," he said, never turning his downtrodden expression away from his newspaper. With her big hazel eyes cast to the floor, she headed to the coffee and began nibbling at her nails, then returned to her own booth to finish some journaling. The coffee shop had good atmosphere. It was one of the few places she could really relax.

Lord, I know you help me make assists every weekend out on the soccer field. Could you help me make this assist? Could you help me assist this man? Everything about him says that he's in desperate need of a friend. She prayed as she opened her bag and dug around for her Bible. It was somewhere in the bottom of her bag. *Boy, I need to clean this thing out!* she thought as she fumbled around to find it and a pen.

Liz played on her college soccer team, and her bag held a lot of stuff: topical pain reliever to rub on sore muscles, an extra pair of socks, a note to her mom, a year's supply of gum, the invitation to an upcoming wedding in which she was to serve as a bridesmaid, a Campus Crusade for Christ tract, and a very special rock. It wasn't a very big rock, but to Liz it held immense weight and meaning.

Small enough to fit into the palm of her hand, the rock reminded her that no matter how capable and successful she became as an athlete and student, she was still dependent upon her Creator. On one side of the rock was inscribed the date, "12-31-00." That was the day she had given her life to Christ. On the other side of the rock was inscribed the word "dependency."

She began her devotions. *You're in control, Lord. Help me help that man.* She read the verse before her: "Do not fear, for I am with you; Do not anxiously look about you, for I am your God. I will strengthen you, surely I will help you" (Isa. 41:10).

Just as she was tearing open a packet of sugar for her coffee, she was interrupted.

"Ahh, miss?"

"Yes," said Liz, surprised. She took her eyes off the packet of sugar she was pouring into her coffee and poured most of the rest of it onto the table.

"Maybe, I could use a refill after all?" His voice was vulnerable.

"I'd be happy to!" Bounding to the self-serve counter, she left her sugary mess and quickly brought a cup to the man's booth.

"Not to sound strange," she said, placing the warm cup on the table before him, "but I'm praying for you." Her chewing gum winked at him from the upper corner of her grin. "It just looks as if you may have had a rough day is all."

She held her breath and waited for his reply. Awkward silence filled the air. She clenched her gum and continued her steadfast grin, the way she did on the soccer field the moment she sent an assist sailing up field. Remembering Isa. 41:10, she waited for his reply.

"I just lost my job, and my wife has left me," said the man as he held the steaming cup in his hands and hung his head in defeat.

"I'm sorry," Liz said, exhaling.

"Me too," he whispered. Thus began an eternity-impacting conversation that lasted for more than an hour. Soon it was time for the man to leave. Slipping back into her own booth, Liz waved goodbye to him. He smiled and gave a nod. His seemed a little less burdened as he headed out the door. She glanced at her Bible still opened to Isaiah. In the skiff of sugar near the base of her coffee cup, she drew a smiley face with her finger. "Thank you, Father," she whispered.

* * *

Jesus stooped down, and with His finger wrote on the ground. But when they persisted in asking Him, He straightened up, and said to them, "He who is without sin among you, let him be the first to throw a stone at her." And again He stooped down, and wrote on the ground *(John 8:6-8)*.

They were ready to stone the woman. They had the law on their side. By rights they could do it and get away with it. An adulterous woman was to be stoned. It was right there in the books. Her fate seemed sealed.

But then someone made an assist. Someone stepped in at the precise moment her life was in the balance. Someone reversed the rolling ball of judgment away from her weary heart and changed her life forever.

Jesus saw her. He came and stooped down with concern. The only thing standing between them and the crowd of raised fists and demanding voices were some simple lines drawn in a skiff of dirt.

Twice the Son of Man scribbled in the dirt. What did

He write? The Bible doesn't say. But it makes you wonder what God in the flesh would *need* to write. Was it a note to his Father? Perhaps. Maybe *You're in control, Father—help me assist this woman. She's in desperate need of a friend.* Whatever was written there in the dirt, it formed a powerful boundary between the woman and the impending doom before her.

One by one, the crowd dropped their stones and left. Those lines in that skiff of dirt were lines of communication between this world and the one above. Those lines in that skiff of dirt were lifelines for a soul that had lost its way. *Thank you, Father,* Jesus prayed as He took the woman's face in his hands and said, "Did no one condemn you?"

"No one, Lord," said the woman as she stood.

"And neither do I," He said as He picked up one of the surrendered stones from the ground and placed it into the palm of her hand.

Empowered by their eternity-impacting conversation and the day's events, she smiled and nodded. Clenching the rock in her fist, she knew she had joined the ranks of those who would follow the Messiah, those who knew how utterly helpless they were without Him. She turned, seeming a little less burdened as she headed home. Never would she forget on whom she depended.

* * *

Some of us are better at making assists than others. Some of us seem to have a built-in radar system that allows us to spot a person in need and know just how to assist, or approach the need of that person without sounding condescending or creating an atmosphere for defensiveness. Those kinds of people are rare.

For those of us who have been lucky enough to know someone like that, it's a taste of heaven. People like that seem to instinctively know not only their own position on the field of life but also their juxtaposition to everyone else's position on the field. With great awareness, they're able to shoot past a few would-be defenders and make an assist when it really counts the most in life. To be consistently effective in that manner with others one must have discernment that comes only from heaven, a discernment so closely matched to His likeness that it must have been chiseled from none other than the Savior himself.

* * *

Every farm kid has the distinct luxury of learning how to drive in the "field." It's a good place to turn a teenager loose behind the wheel. There's not a lot to hit out there in the wide-open patches on a farm.

"That's the jake-brake," my dad instructed after quickly orienting me to the gears of the semi-truck. I guess he felt that as long as I knew how to stop the thing, I was safe. Since he had only one son and a lot of acres to harvest, when I was a teenager I became Dad's other "guy" in the field. I loved the fact that he trusted me enough to allow me to drive such a big rig. I enjoyed driving the truck every summer when harvest rolled around.

Mainly because of Wilbur.

Though in his 70s, Wilbur was spry. He drove a truck, too, and could hop up and down to and from the cab as if he were still a kid. I considered him a second grandpa. But more than that, he was a friend to me—a friend to everyone, really. He just knew how to read people.

"Good morning, Sunshine," he would say with a grin so as to annoy me in my sleepy-eyed, zombie teen-state. I would laugh, knowing I was anything but sunshine in the morning.

In the afternoons as we waited for a dump from the combine, we parked our trucks and visited, and then out of nowhere he would say, "Look—do you see him?" Squinting, I would spend forever looking in the same direction but never see what it was he was seeing. Then some small movement would unlock the mystery. There, tucked into a thick underbrush, a deer grazed.

After a while I gave Wilbur the nickname Radar. It was a fair trade for Sunshine. He really did have a heavenly discernment about him. He listened twice as much as he talked. Maybe that was it. He knew how to make assists in simple conversation. He lightened the mood with humor or by the simple act of handing a wrench to someone at just the right time. Somehow he read the lives of those around him with chiseled precision. Nothing seemed to slip by him—not a person, not an animal. It made him unforgettable.

In this hurry-up world of demanding jobs and full

schedules, most people don't seem to have the time it takes to be that discerning in every situation with every person they run into. Most don't even take the time to ask for that kind of heavenly wisdom. On the other hand, animals have all the time in the world and seem to be better at discerning the needs around them—more so than this busy world full of busy people never glancing up from their coffee cups.

Animals were created with built-in radar that allows them to discern their surroundings. Hippopotamuses, for example, when lounging in marshes and shallow pools of water, can hear activity both above water as well as under water. With their eyes and ears above the water line, they are able to take in the rustling of nearby crocs and other noises. Below the water, their submerged jawbones conduct sound waves, allowing them to hear any movement that might indicate danger lurking in the waters.

Elephants have the same kind of infrasound hearing. It baffles scientists. Elephants can routinely know the whereabouts of other elephants several miles away. In fact, they have the ability to hear distress sounds up to 9.8 miles away.

Recently the news reported that a man was out surfing when he was attacked by a shark. Biting into his torso, the shark was ready to rip a chunk away from his body, except for the fact that it couldn't bite through the surf board beneath the man. The shark let go, leaving him in a pool of blood as it circled back around for a better angle at which to attack the man.

Just when it seemed the shark would have him for

dinner, a pod of dolphins, sensing the man was in need of help, arrayed themselves in the water, creating a circle around him as he paddled his way to the shoreline.

* * *

I wonder if a bridesmaid can get away with chewing gum, she thought as she paced herself behind one of the other runners and blew a bubble. Her roommate's wedding was just two months away. The only dress she ever felt really good in was the $300 dollar prom dress she begged her dad to buy for her when she was in high school. She remembered the way he looked at her when she appeared around the corner of the family room to greet her date. Her dad didn't need to say a word. That look on his face told her she was his princess. *Bless my dad today, Lord,* she prayed smiling through the overcast Seattle weather.

Puddles from the night before lapped at her shins as she and her running mates continued the jog along the sidewalk.

"Happy early birthday, Liz," panted one of her fellow joggers in front of her.

"Don't make me feel old!" Liz quipped as she looked at her watch to note their pace. It was 9:15 A.M. Her birthday was in three days. She thought about her family back home in Richland. She knew her mom would pick up a vanilla cake with raspberry filling and butter cream frosting. *You go, girl—Mom! Thank you, Lord, for the gift of my family and friends.*

She knew Lindsey would give her a call and wish her in the dorkiest voice possible a "Happwee Birfdee!" on her answering machine. It would only be fair, after all the ranting messages *she* left on *Lindsey's* answering machine. They had a ridiculously silly friendship, the kind that allowed them to laugh until they cried, until they split their sides. It was as if they had their own language. *How do I thank you for her, Lord? She opened my eyes to you!*

Nearing a light post, Liz slowed to a walk, then stopped. It felt good to breathe deeply. She wiped her brow, and with thoughts of her family and friends and her favorite cake, she blew one last bubble—and was gone.

Gone. In a matter of seconds, a Pontiac Grand Am screamed up onto the sidewalk and ran over Liz where she stood several feet back from the curb. The impact sheered the light pole near Liz and sent the steel bar pummeling down on top of her—a fatal blow.

* * *

Each bridesmaid wore a silver necklace with a tiny silver running shoe on a chain. Each groomsman had a running shoe tied up in his boutonniere. The sanctuary was beautiful, filled with family and friends. The dresses were perfect. The flowers were perfect. It was a perfect day except for the gap between two of the bridesmaids—the place Liz was to have stood.

Just shy of her 27th birthday, Goliath had come out of nowhere and cut her down. A thousand people had gone to her funeral. Family and friends and coworkers from Brooks Sports, where Liz had worked, talked about the way she came alongside people, even strangers, and touched them with her smile and her concern for them. Her discerning heart "saw" people—especially the people the world was too busy to notice. In her honor, the company she worked for designed a thousand shoes with Liz's initials on them and appropriately named the line "The Defiance."

It summed up the way Liz lived. When her body felt like quitting, she pushed another mile in defiance. When she didn't feel like being vulnerable and reaching out to someone at the coffee shop, in defiance of her comfort-seeking flesh, she reached out in faith anyway.

"We know what Liz would say to that 16-year-old girl behind the wheel of the Pontiac Grand Am," said her mother, who faces life without her daughter. "She would wrap her arms around her and tell her how much God loves her."

As the wedding march played and the candles were lit, the family imagined Liz in her dress. She would have had wad of gum tucked out of sight in the corner of that beautiful smile of hers and maybe even a pair of running shoes out of sight under her dress. Surely their missing bridesmaid would smile and tell them that there wasn't time to be complacent—after all, life's short. Run long. They knew she would want them to grab their sneakers and go make some eternity-impacting assists. They knew she would want them to tell others about the distance a King ran to call them His own. And when they did, they knew she would thrust her fists into the darkness and yell "Score!"

Cattle Company

Beneath Bethlehem's starlight, where shepherds kneel, having left costly flocks in field, and where earthly kings spared no journeying expense to bow in reverence,
There lay a newborn King around which wise men still rejoice and sing of His great sacrificial knee for all humanity.

From royal robes
to swaddling clothes—
He bowed His head and knelt.

From palatial chambers
to the cradle of a cattle's trough—
He bowed His head and knelt.

From a regal crown
to a thorny wreath gathered round—
He bowed His head and knelt.

From the splendor of a vast kingdom
to the darkness of a damp
and borrowed tomb—
He bowed His head and knelt.

O manger wherein I cringe to see my Savior take such a costly knee, among your company bid me no welcome 'til at your door the failings of my heart be frisked,
lest the King should find on bended knee

a heart little more than that of the kneeling cattle grazing before Him with appetites of indifference.

—Jody

AFTERWORD

It's some of the most beautiful glass in the world. The pieces are called fulgurites, and they come in all different shapes and sizes. There is no other glass quite like it. It's so beautiful and unique that some people wear it for jewelry; others use it as decorative pieces in their china closets. It's made only one way: when lightning strikes sand.

Life is full of lightning strikes.

Only the Habakkuk heart allows God to take those deadly strikes and turn them into something beautiful. Only the Habakkuk heart stands yielded in a storm and keeps its hope when the storm grows worse. For it is a heart that trusts in Jesus Christ, who had more to lose than any of us and gave it all up for us. It's a heart whose unconditional worship jewels the earth and allows others to dimly see through a glass the goodness of God. Even when Goliath doesn't fall.

SCRIPTURES OF HOPE

"We know that God causes all things to work together for good to those who love God, to those who are called according to His purpose" (Rom. 8:28).

"The LORD will accomplish what concerns me" (Ps. 138:8).

"We are afflicted in every way, but not crushed; perplexed, but not despairing; persecuted, but not forsaken; struck down, but not destroyed" (2 Cor. 4:8-9).

"The eyes of the LORD move to and fro throughout the earth that He may strongly support those whose heart is completely His" (2 Chron. 16:9).

"Consider it pure joy, my brothers, whenever you face trials of many kinds, because you know that the testing of your faith develops perseverance. Perseverance must finish its work so that you may be mature and complete, not lacking anything. If any of you lacks wisdom, he should ask God, who gives generously to all without finding fault. But when he asks, he must believe and not doubt, because he who doubts is like the wave of the sea, blown and tossed by the wind. That man should not think he will receive anything from the Lord; he is a double-minded man, unstable in all he does" (James 1:2-8, NIV).

Be anxious for nothing, but in everything by prayer and supplication with thanksgiving let your requests be made known to God. And the peace of God, which surpasses all comprehension, will guard your hearts and your minds in Christ Jesus" (Phil. 4:6-7).

"Trust in the LORD with all your heart And do not lean on your own understanding" (Prov. 3:5).

"Whatever is true, whatever is honorable, whatever is right, whatever is pure, whatever is lovely, whatever is of good repute, if there is any excellence and if anything worthy of praise, dwell on these things . . . and the God of peace will be with you" (Phil. 4:8-9).

"I consider that the sufferings of this present time are not worthy to be compared with the glory that is to be revealed to us (Rom. 8:18).

"We count those blessed who endured. You have heard of the endurance of Job and have seen the outcome of the Lord's dealings, that the Lord is full of compassion and is merciful (James 5:11).

"He who keeps you will not slumber" (Ps. 121:3).

"At my first defense no one supported me, but all deserted me; may it not be counted against them. But the Lord stood with me and strengthened me, so that through me the proclamation might be fully accomplished" (2 Tim. 4:16-17).

"Those who sow in tears shall reap with joyful shouting" (Ps. 126:5).

"If I dwell in the remotest part of the sea, Even there Your hand will lead me" (Ps. 139:9-10).

"Therefore, humble yourselves under the mighty hand of God, that He may exalt you at the proper time, casting all your anxiety on Him, because He cares for you. Be of sober spirit, be on the alert. Your adversary, the devil, prowls around like a roaring lion, seeking someone to devour. But resist him, firm in your faith, knowing that the same experiences of suffering are being accomplished by your brethren who are in the world. After you have suffered for a little while, the God of all grace, who called you to His eternal glory in Christ, will Himself perfect, confirm, strengthen and establish you" (1 Pet. 5:6-10).

"Even though I walk through the valley of the shadow of death, I will fear no evil, for You are with me. Your rod and Your staff, they comfort me. You prepare a table before me in the presence of my enemies; You have anointed my head with oil; my cup overflows" (Ps. 23:4-5).

"Once God has spoken; Twice I have heard this: That power belongs to God; and lovingkindness is Yours, O LORD, For you recompense a man according to his work" (Ps. 62:11-12).

"Put on the full armor of God, that you may be able to stand firm against the schemes of the devil. For our struggle is not against flesh and blood, but against the rulers, against the powers, against the world forces of this darkness, against the spiritual forces of wickedness in the heavenly places" (Eph. 6:11-12).

"I count all things to be loss in view of the surpassing value of knowing Christ Jesus my Lord, for whom I have suffered the loss of all things, and count them but rubbish so that I may gain Christ" (Phil. 3:8).

"This hope we have as an anchor of the soul, a hope both sure and steadfast and one which enters within the veil" (Heb. 6:19).

"Who will separate us from the love of Christ? Will tribulation, or distress, or persecution, or famine, or nakedness, or peril, or sword? . . . Neither death, nor life, nor angels, nor principalities, nor things present, nor things to come, nor powers, nor height, nor depth, nor any other created thing, will be able to separate us from the love of God, which is in Christ Jesus our Lord" (Rom. 8:35, 38-39).

"Set your mind on the things above, not on the things that are on earth. For you have died and your life is hidden with Christ in God. When Christ, who is our life, is revealed, then you also will be revealed with Him in glory" (Col. 3:2-4).

"The Lord is faithful, and He will strengthen and protect you from the evil one" (2 Thess. 3:3).

"Fixing our eyes on Jesus, the author and perfecter of faith, who for the joy set before Him endured the cross, despising the shame, and has sat down at the right hand of the throne of God" (Heb. 12:2).

"However, as it is written: No eye has seen, no ear has heard, no mind has conceived what God has prepared for those who love him" (1 Cor. 2:9, NIV).

"May mercy and peace and love be multiplied to you" (Jude 2).

"As for me, I will watch expectantly for the LORD; I will wait for the God of my salvation. My God will hear me. Do not rejoice over me, O my enemy. Though I fall I will rise; Though I dwell in darkness, the LORD is a light for me" (Micah 7:7-8).

"You, O LORD, are a shield about me, my glory, and the One who lifts my head" (Ps. 3:3).

"To this one I will look, To him who is humble and contrite of spirit, and who trembles at My word" (Isa. 66:2).

"He who dwells in the shelter of the Most High Will abide in the shadow of the Almighty. I will say to the LORD, 'My refuge and my fortress, My God, in whom I trust!'" (Ps. 91:1-2).

"I will give thanks to the LORD with all my heart, In the company of the upright and in the assembly. Great are the works of the LORD; They are studied by all who delight in them" (Ps. 111:1-2).

"This hope we have as an anchor of the soul, a hope both sure and steadfast and one which enters within the veil, where Jesus has entered as a forerunner for us, having become a high priest forever according to the order of Melchizedek" (Heb. 6:19-20).

"When I remember You on my bed, I meditate on You in the night watches" (Ps. 63:6).

"God is opposed to the proud, but gives grace to the humble" (James 4:6).

WORKS CITED

Braveheart, 1995. Written by Randall Wallace; directed by Mel Gibson. Paramount Pictures.

Coppedge, David. "The World's Greatest Creation Scientists." <http://www.creationsafaris.com>

"Good News from Israel." <http://newsoftheday>

"Seward's Folly, The Purchase of Alaska." <http://www.u-s-history.com/pages/h230.html>

Weisberger, Bernard. *Statue of Liberty: The First Hundred Years.* New York: American Heritage, 1985.

An honest look at the frustration of waiting . . .
it's about time.

Examine the mysteries of God's timing and learn to transform the frustration of waiting into a positive force that will enrich and change your life.

When God Takes Too Long
Learning to Thrive During Life's Delays
By Joseph Bentz

ISBN-13: 978-0-8341-2218-5

Available wherever Christian books are sold.

Are you discouraged

with the way

your life is going?

In *When Life Doesn't Turn Out the Way You Expect,* Jerry Brecheisen and Lawrence Wilson indentify the negative effects of difficult life experiences and bring you to the point of healing the hurts and disappointments. You will relate to the stories of heartbreak, loss, rejection, and failure that parallel the authors' own difficult life experiences. Then they guide you to the point of healing–the place where God brings redemption to suffering.

 Look for it wherever Christian books are sold!

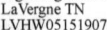

www.ingramcontent.com/pod-product-compliance
Lightning Source LLC
LaVergne TN
LVHW051519070426
835507LV00023B/3202